Essential Guides for
EARLY CAREER
TEACHERS

Professional
Behaviours

Jen,

Your organisation and focus will get you far!... and of course your passion for teaching! well done, and lucky Heybridge!

from the TKAT SCITT Team.

Essential Guides for Early Career Teachers

The *Essential Guides for Early Career Teachers* provide accessible, carefully researched, quick-reads for early career teachers, covering the key topics you will encounter during your training year and first two years of teaching. They complement and are fully in line with the new *Early Career Framework* and are intended to assist ongoing professional development by bringing together current information and thinking on each area in one convenient place. The texts are edited by Emma Hollis, Executive Director of the National Association of School-Based Teacher Trainers (NASBTT), who brings a wealth of experience, expertise and knowledge to the series.

Why not explore the other books in this series?

*Essential Guides for Early Career Teachers: **Assessment***
Alys Finch
Paperback ISBN: 978-1-912508-93-8

*Essential Guides for Early Career Teachers: **Mental Well-being and Self Care***
Sally Price
Paperback ISBN: 978-1-912508-97-6

*Essential Guides for Early Career Teachers: **Special Educational Needs and Disability***
Anita Devi
Paperback ISBN: 978-1-913063-29-0

*Essential Guides for Early Career Teachers: **Understanding and Developing Positive Behaviour in Schools***
Patrick Garton
Paperback ISBN: 978-1-913453-09-1

*Essential Guides for Early Career Teachers: **Using Cognitive Science in the Classroom***
Kelly Woodford-Richens
Paperback ISBN: 978-1-914171-05-5

*Essential Guides for Early Career Teachers: **Workload – Taking Ownership of your Teaching***
Julie Greer
Paperback ISBN: 978-1-913453-41-1

Our titles are also available in a range of electronic formats. To order, or for details of our bulk discounts, please go to our website www.criticalpublishing.com or contact our distributor, Ingram Publisher Services (IPS UK), 10 Thornbury Road, Plymouth PL6 7PP, telephone 01752 202301 or email IPSUK.orders@ingramcontent.com.

CRITICAL
PUBLISHING

Essential Guides for
EARLY CAREER
TEACHERS

Professional
Behaviours

NASBTT

Colin Howard and Rachael Paige
Series editor: Emma Hollis

First published in 2022 by Critical Publishing Ltd

British Library Cataloguing in Publication Data
A CIP record for this book is available from the British Library

ISBN: 978-1-915080-16-5

This book is also available in the following e-book formats:

EPUB ISBN: 978-1-915080-17-2
Adobe e-book ISBN: 978-1-915080-18-9

The rights of Colin Howard and Rachael Paige to be identified as the Authors of this work have been asserted by them in accordance with the Copyright, Design and Patents Act 1988.

Cartoon illustrations by Élisabeth Eudes-Pascal represented by GCI

Cover and text design by Out of House Limited
Project management by Newgen Publishing UK
Printed and bound in Great Britain by 4edge, Essex

Critical Publishing
3 Connaught Road
St Albans
AL3 5RX

www.criticalpublishing.com

Printed on FSC accredited paper

Contents

Meet the series editor

Emma Hollis

I am Executive Director of the NASBTT (National Association of School-Based Teacher Trainers) and my absolute passion is teacher education. After gaining a first-class degree in psychology I trained as a primary teacher, and soon became head of initial teacher training for a School Centred Initial Teacher Training (SCITT) provider. I am dedicated to ensuring teachers are given access to high-quality professional development at the early stages of and throughout their careers.

Meet the authors

Colin Howard

I am an associate lecturer in initial teacher education at the University of Worcester. I have been involved in primary education for over 30 years and have been a successful headteacher in both small village and large primary settings. My research interests link to primary science, mentoring trainees, school leadership, Special Educational Needs and Disabilities (SEND) and teacher professional identity. I have written publications associated with primary science, teachers' and students' mental health and well-being, British Values, mentoring in schools and school leadership and management. I am dedicated to mentoring and supporting students to become outstanding teachers of the future.

Rachael Paige

I have worked in primary education for over 20 years as a headteacher of a Church of England primary school before moving into teacher education and training. My work in school focused on inclusion through my Special Educational Needs Co-ordinator (SENCo) role and leading English and music. One of the key projects I led in school focused on the implementation of a new positive behaviour approach through distributed leadership. I am currently the Head of Department for Primary Education at the University of Worcester, ensuring that new and established teachers are supported in their own development and given opportunities to think in creative and critical ways. My key research area is teacher presence and I have also written about developing teacher identity for trainee teachers, how leadership approaches can enable the development of the whole child, and relational leadership to create positive climates for schools.

Acknowledgements

We would like to thank all those who have influenced the ideas in this book.

Special thanks to Ben King, Stephen Slinn, Hannah Elliott and Laura Slinn for their mentoring insights.

A note about examples and case studies

Although many of the examples and case studies throughout the book focus on the primary age phase, they are equally applicable in principle to the secondary age phase. For example, as in Chapter 1's case study, the development of teacher identity and the advice provided by Paul is not age phase specific. It will be influenced by your context, your own values and narratives. Similarly, in Chapter 4 the case study regarding Reggie is about developing relationships, working with others and reflecting on your own needs. This transcends age phase.

Remember that whatever age phase you may find yourself in, the notion of teacher identity, the need to develop professionally, seeking advice and support from colleagues and looking after yourself will be of paramount importance if you are to thrive in your newly chosen profession.

Foreword

As a passionate advocate of high-quality teacher education and continuing professional development (CPD), it had always been a source of frustration for me that, historically, beyond the Initial Teacher Training (ITT) year, access to high-quality, structured ongoing professional development was always something of a lottery for teachers. Access to high-quality support was patchy, with some schools and local authorities offering fantastic opportunities for teachers throughout their careers while in other locations, CPD was given lip service at best and, at worst, was non-existent.

This series was conceived to attempt to close some of those gaps and to offer accessible professional learning to busy teachers in the early stages of their careers. It was therefore a moment of genuine pleasure when the proposals for an entitlement for all early career teachers (ECTs) to receive a package of support, guidance and education first landed on my desk. Through the Early Career Framework, there is now a genuine opportunity for school communities to work together to offer the very best early career development for our most precious of resources – the teachers in our schools.

The aim of this series is to distil some of the key topics which occupy the thoughts of early career teachers into digestible, informative texts which will promote discussion, contemplation and reflection and will spark further exploration into practice. In each edition, you will find a series of practical suggestions for how you can put the 'big idea' in each chapter into practice: now, next week and in the long term. By offering opportunities to bring the learning into the classroom in a very concrete way, we hope to help embed many of the principles we share into your day-to-day teaching.

As you embark on your career as an early career teacher, there is much that you must learn, assimilate and put into practice but you will quickly find that there is nothing more important or more fundamental to your professional identity as a teacher than the professional behaviours you develop, nurture and demonstrate both now and throughout your entire career. Teaching is much more than a job; it has the potential to be the most rewarding experience of your life. Paying close attention to the professional you want to be right from the very start gives you the best opportunity to enjoy a long lasting and well-balanced professionally and personally rewarding career. This title offers straightforward, helpful, actionable advice to start you in this lifelong journey.

I hope you enjoy reading it as much as I have enjoyed editing it.

Emma Hollis
Executive Director, NASBTT

Chapter 1   All about you: the professional self

What? (The big idea)

Develop your unique identity

As you will realise, every teacher is unique and brings something specific to their classroom through their characteristics, dispositions and interests. This chapter will help you consider your own authenticity as you develop your teacher identity. Teaching is often referred to as an act or a performance (Hart, 2007); however, in this chapter we consider teaching to be a more complex task which requires investment of the authentic self (Meijer et al, 2009). It begins by asking you to consider how your own sense of identity as a teacher is developing and has evolved. To start in this way may feel strange: in your professional life you will be thinking about other people and things for much of the time – the children in your class and their families, your colleagues and other external agencies and, of course, ensuring that the learning environment is as good as it can be. Often there is little time for you to reflect upon what you are like professionally and how this self is developing. This chapter demonstrates why developing your own sense of identity and professional self is important for success.

Through exploration of the notion of identity and the professional self, this chapter helps you consider how your values and sense of purpose in teaching are

Note: In this chapter, Rachael Paige reflects on some aspects of her professional development and therefore first-person references relate to her experience.

important foundations in your early career and beyond. The alignment between your own values and the school culture in which you work will be explored so that you are able to flourish within your setting. A key idea is that professional identity develops over time (Akkerman and Meijer, 2011) and can be influenced by situations and context (Day et al, 2006). This is a positive idea to consider as it offers opportunity and possibility for what you could become in your teaching career as you gain experience and develop as a teacher.

You are starting out on an exciting and rewarding journey in teaching and you will learn along the way from others, from experiences and through engagement with evidence-based research. As part of your routine, take the time to reflect upon what you are learning from these sources and how this is shaping you as a professional. Kornelsen (2006, p 79) talks about shifting from a 'way of doing to a way of being' as you develop in confidence as a teacher. In your early career you may feel like you are simply 'doing' without that sense of bringing something of yourself to the classroom (Meijer et al, 2009): what you might consider the *comfortableness* of teaching, where being in the teacher role is played out easily and naturally for you. When you start thinking about the development of your professional identity you will realise how far-reaching the impact is upon the success you will have in school because your sense of who you are and the values you hold will be lived out in your behaviours and attitudes. Your sense of identity, expressed outwardly in your behaviours and attitudes, is influenced by the balance of the personal, professional and situational dimensions which Day et al (2006) found in their study. As you develop an understanding of the importance of how teacher identity will show itself in the interactions you have with others and the way you behave in your school context, you can begin to understand that these aspects impact the success you are having in your role. Canrinus et al (2012) argue that this success is seen in job satisfaction, motivation, self-efficacy and commitment. So, you can see that taking time to consider your teacher identity and professional self is not a self-indulgent exercise but potentially crucial for success and in supporting a positive early career experience.

So what? ◀◀◀

Developing your professional identity

Let's start to think about some of these ideas and consider what difference this makes to you in your teacher role and the impact this will have upon your practice and ultimately the children in your classroom. In this section you will consider how your values and beliefs shape your teacher identity, influencing your behaviours and attitudes, which consequently impact your success and outcomes.

Day et al's (2006) dimensions of professional, personal and situational in the construction of professional self and identity will be used to support the exploration of this notion.

Take some time to think about what it is that you value about working in education. What is it that is motivating you to work with children and their families in a school context? For me, I have always had a belief that education brings opportunities and possibilities. Being the first generation in my family to go to university and obtain a degree reinforces for me how education has enabled me in both my professional and personal life. To extend this idea, the belief that education should be accessible for all integrates values around inclusion, diversity, fairness and ethical behaviours. Some of these ideas may overlap with your values and beliefs about why education is important and why you are committing your professional life to this venture. You may have some other motivators, but what you will notice is that these values and beliefs drive the way you behave and interact with others. If you are more consciously aware of these values and beliefs, then you will be more mindful of the decisions you are making and the actions you are taking. For example, if you are to live out a belief that education should be accessible for all, how would you ensure that you are creating an environment in your classroom so that all children are engaged, motivated and inspired? How do your relationships with parents and carers demonstrate that you are inclusive and committed to ensuring all children in your class can flourish? How do you ensure that the curriculum you are teaching is diverse and representative? You can see already that by taking some time to understand who you are and who you want to be in terms of your own professional identity is important and can impact on many aspects of your work. This approach also supports the view that our identity is not fixed but evolves over time. O'Connor (2008) supports this perspective, explaining that professional identity is how your personal beliefs, values and philosophies are lived out in actions and behaviours and, while some values hold fast over time, some can evolve and change over time, too.

Day et al's (2006) work has been referred to already in this chapter and the intention is to use this work as a structure to support your thinking about this subject. The three dimensions (personal, professional and situational) can be considered separately but they also interlink and, when viewed as interconnecting dimensions, there is a greater sense of the teacher bringing something authentic and unique to the classroom experience. Meijer et al (2009) talk about a meeting of the personal and professional which culminates in the presence that you create in the classroom, which is unique to each teacher. Certainly, my own research on teacher presence reinforces that each teacher needs to find their own sense of themselves in the classroom: what I term *comfortableness* (Paige et al, 2020). Let's explore these dimensions and consider their application for you as an ECT.

Personal dimension

When you consider your personal identity, this can be influenced by many factors and is multi-layered. Your own social, religious and cultural background may influence the way you view the world and the way you interact. This may also align you to certain philosophies which will shape your thinking and behaviours. The experiences you have had, too, influence your view of yourself and the world around you. The personal dimension could be thought of as who you are when not in the professional spheres, without the restrictions of professional expectations or rules. It incorporates your interests and hobbies and your engagement with things that make you happy. It also includes your characteristics and dispositions that emerge as part of your personality. For some teachers, this personal dimension exists separately from their professional persona but other teachers bring parts of this dimension to their classroom work. Many studies (for example, Day et al, 2006; O'Connor, 2008; Meijer et al, 2009) argue that bringing together something of your personal self with your professional self supports positive outcomes for you as the teacher (in terms of being happy in your role) and in developing positive relationships with the children in your classroom. To think of this simply, it is the *comfortableness* introduced earlier where you are not pretending or acting out a role, but you are able to bring your own personality and interests to the classroom. In my work on teacher presence, participants in my study spoke about what I call 'an exaggerated self', that is, being yourself so that there is genuine and authentic engagement with children, but certain actions and behaviours may be deliberately exaggerated or emphasised as an approach to establish teacher presence that is influential and impactful in the classroom (Paige et al, 2020).

Professional dimension

Our professional identity is influenced by our personal identity, which has been presented as multi-layered with our affinity to different groups, philosophies, interests and experiences. O'Connor (2008) found that there are aspects of the personal self that are brought to the professional sphere which are expressions of who you are, as an individual, and there may be some aspects that are chosen to be exaggerated more than others. However, there will also be aspects of the personal that are chosen to be repressed. This is an interesting idea, that you can shape your professional identity based upon your personal dimension, but in such a way that will meet the needs of the context (or situation) in which you are placed.

In terms of your professional self, there are expectations and parameters distinguished through professional standards as well as national and school policy which will influence your behaviour and attitudes to your work. You will also be aware of the hierarchy within your school and your place within that hierarchy, which will also change over your career. Your perceptions, too, will influence your professional identity in terms of how well you think you are doing in your new career. Nias (2014) has written some interesting and emotive work around how much investment of the self by the individual is brought in to teaching, and how the successes and less successful experiences can influence the teacher's perception of themselves and their professional identity. This is where the role of your ECT mentor is extremely important in supporting you to make sense of the experiences you are having: good and not so good. Palombo and Daly (2021) present an argument for educative mentoring which moves away from the 'expert-novice' approach where you may be encouraged to replicate what your mentor finds effective or practice that is common in your school. Rather, it is a developmental process (Howard et al, 2020), where your mentor supports you in exploring your own developing philosophy and beliefs about learning and teaching. Palombo and Daly (2021) describe this approach as unsettling because beliefs and practices will develop and shift over time. There is not necessarily a sense of meeting expectations, but more of developing a reflexive approach to your professional life.

The more you consider this professional dimension and engage with the ideas around a developing identity, you should start to recognise that what you are experiencing or feeling now is not necessarily how you will view your professional self in the future. You will hear the idea of 'surviving' and 'thriving' in your early career and this idea of surviving in a new and complex teaching environment is widely accepted as the experience of many new teachers. However, in the context of your professional identity and who you think you are in the professional context, surviving may not be a helpful expression, even if acknowledged as a real experience of many ECTs. Consider your current state as part of your development and recognise that your professional identity is evolving as you develop through experiences and your engagement with evidence-based practice. To adopt this view of your professional self as developing and evolving is a positive approach, and ensuring that you have a strong foundation of your own personal views will bring some certainty when you will be learning a lot and may feel uncertain at times.

Situational dimension

An idea from Day et al's (2006) work is that identity becomes more or less stable at different times based upon aspects such as situational context. It is also important to recognise that these dimensions are also fluid, and each may have more or less impact upon the individual at different times. As an ECT moving to your first teaching post you may or may not have considered how well your own values and beliefs align with those of your school context. When attending interviews, it is important for you to consider that while the panel are evaluating your performance in relation to the post at their school, you are also evaluating how the school aligns with your own educational philosophy and your understanding of components that build a positive learning community. When there is a synthesis between your ethos and the school culture, you will gain a greater sense of being part of that community, actively participating and contributing to an overall positive climate for learning.

We could explore many ways that context and situations can influence identity (both positive and negative), and the case study below will help to explore this aspect. A key consideration for you is how to ensure that you have a strong foundation based in your values and beliefs, which will ensure that your professional behaviours and interactions reflect the person you want to be: that is, reflect your identity and the professional self you desire to portray. The reflective task for you to engage with next is designed to help you do this.

A way of recognising your developing identity

We do not always appreciate how we change over time or even take the time to celebrate our own resilience and accomplishments. When I first became a headteacher I used journaling to manage my feelings and to make sense of some of the new experiences and situations I was managing. I have kept these journals as a way to acknowledge how I have developed as a leader and to recognise that I was able to withstand and even flourish in challenging situations. I will admit, I find some of the entries embarrassing now and I can see my own naivety, but those experiences, thoughts, feelings and perceptions have shaped who I am now and how I manage those different dimensions we explored earlier in this chapter.

In this reflective activity, the intention is to capture the 'here and now' of your experience and what is motivating you to be a teacher and commit to this rewarding profession. You will then have opportunity in the future to reflect on what has remained the same for you (perhaps your values) and what has changed (perhaps your comfortableness in your role).

Reflective task ◀◀◀

Write a letter to your future self to be opened in a year's time about why you have chosen to be a teacher, what has motivated you and what kind of teacher you want to be. Identify the characteristics and skills you already hold now and explain where you want to develop.

Reflect on how things are for you now, in this early part of your career. What is going well? What are the challenges? How are you responding to the balancing of the professional, personal and situational/contextual dimensions that Day et al (2006) describe?

Finish your letter by identifying how you will ensure that you can hold on to your values and motivations, even in difficult times. You could ask yourself: are you where you planned to be?

Now seal your letter and put it somewhere safe. Set a reminder on your calendar for a year's time to open the letter.

Case study ◀◀◀

Teacher presence

Paul had spent 20 years in the military and had progressed in his career to training other soldiers. He had decided to move into primary teaching and anticipated bringing many skills and experiences into his new career. This extract is part of a reflection five years after he had gained his Post-Graduate Certificate of Education (PGCE). He reflects on how he felt he had to 'take off' his military identity, which included his own sense of achievement and self-esteem through the many successes he had enjoyed, and to start to re-build his own sense of who he is in this new professional situation. His own values remained strong, and he describes how this helped him through a very challenging first year where personally he was unhappy and questioning his own professional identity. He talks about how he is now able to apply his own philosophy and experiences in his mentoring roles with new teachers.

Paul's view of identity, reflecting upon his own first year in teaching

During my first year I was so frightened of letting the children run and me losing control of their behaviour. I had a challenging class and I was put straight in to Year 6. There were many complex needs and situations for the children that I was managing, as well as learning about being in charge of my own class. And I was terrified to give them an inch in case they took a mile. So, I was quite strict with them. More than I should have been, which meant that I never really built up a rapport with them at all. I made massive mistakes in my relationships with the children in my class as well as around just enjoying being with the children in my class. This was a key area I did not want to repeat in the future. I really wasn't happy and so my decisions about how I was going to be in the classroom as a professional was impacting my own personal happiness.

The next year I reflected upon what had happened and thought: right, let's start again. Let's see what I did right? I admitted to myself my own shortcomings, too. I realised I needed to worry less about what others thought I should be in terms of becoming a 'teacher' and worry more about building a safe, supportive and inspiring environment for the children. And quickly I could see my own identity developing from those reflections. What my strength is now I would say was my weakness in my first year. So, it does come. You just have to take the time to reflect, to read, to observe, and to start to become comfortable in your own skin. I had a very difficult transition because I was very institutionalised from my previous career. And J was literally having to take off a helmet and put on a mortar board.

Paul's view of identity as a mentor

I would say to any new teachers to be yourself, learn your own strengths and learn your own weaknesses, because if you know your strengths and weaknesses you can play to them. Don't try and mimic someone else. Which I think is a failure of many new teachers in as much that they look at the teachers they go in with and they try and do what they do, thinking that is the right way. Actually, it might not necessarily be the right way for the new teacher. And I don't necessarily think there is a right and wrong way. So, I think, the key thing I would say to my mentee (and this is something I am working on myself, too) is look at what you are good at, what works for you, look at other people, find something you like, try it; if it doesn't work and it doesn't fit you and the class doesn't like it, try something else. And what you do with one class might not work with another class, so always be open to reflect on your own practice and tweak your own practice. It's not necessarily the class that has to change; in some cases, it is you.

Now what? ◀ ◀ ◀

Practical ways to identify professional identity

As this topic of developing your professional self and how this interlinks with your sense of identity has been explored in the chapter, the skill of reflexive practice is emerging as a key professional skill to adopt. You will have explored models of reflection in your Initial Teacher Training (ITT) programme and you may have considered how the concept of reflexive practice as taking a critical view of your practice and considering the actions you will take as a consequence of that consideration influences your developing role. This reflexive approach is evident in the case study shared with you and offers a practical example of reflexivity in practice. The practical tasks below offer opportunity, in a staged and progressive way, for you to engage in some reflexive practice considering what you are observing, experiencing and learning from your engagement with evidence and research and making sense of all this with the mentoring and coaching support of your ECT mentor.

Practical task for tomorrow ◀◀◀

- Observe and notice teachers in your school who seem to have a confidence and comfortableness about them. Can you identify how they may have brought together their personal and professional self to create a teacher identity?

- Thinking about Paul's advice in the case study, consider how this might apply to you as you bring together those personal and professional aspects.

Practical task for next week ◀◀◀

- Talk with your ECT mentor about how your own sense of identity is developing as a teacher. Do you feel like a teacher or are you having a sense of 'imposter syndrome'? Unpick with your mentor what is helping you feel confident in your identity and in which areas you are feeling less confident.

- Set yourself some personal actions and goals to help build your confidence and experience in these areas.

Practical task for the long term ◀◀◀

- At the end of your first year as an ECT, use your letter from the reflective task to reflect upon how much you have developed and changed.

- You could use this letter as a prompt for a professional dialogue with your mentor.

- Make a list of the strategies you have developed to help you through the challenges and build upon these as you move forward in your career.

What next? ◀ ◀ ◀

This chapter set out to explore how you are developing your professional identity. Throughout the chapter a key message is to give value to the unique characteristics you bring and also to encourage you to develop genuine and authentic ways of behaving and interacting in your school environment. There is a collective understanding in the teaching community that the first few years can be challenging ('survival') with lots of things to learn and the new responsibility of having your own class. Remember that your identity, sense of self and own confidence and comfortableness in your role are developing, changing and evolving. Taking a step at a time will support you in ensuring that all of these aspects are manageable while still ensuring that you are progressing forward in your developing sense of who you are as a teacher.

Further reading

Evans, L (1998) *Teacher Morale, Job Satisfaction and Motivation*. London: Cassells.

Jacklin, A, Griffith, V and Robinson, C (2006) *Beginning Primary Teaching: Moving Beyond Surviving*. Maidenhead: Open University Press.

Roberts, L (2000) Shifting Identities: An Investigation into Student and Novice Teachers' Evolving Professional Identity. *Journal of Education for Teaching*, 26(2): 185-6.

Townsend, A and Kington, A (2020) Teachers' Professional Identity and Self-efficacy: A Study of Teachers with 4-7 Years of Experience. In Kington, A and Blackmore, K (eds) *Social and Learning Relationships in Primary Education* (pp 139-56). London: Bloomsbury.

References

Akkerman, S and Meijer, P (2011) A Dialogic Approach to Conceptualizing Teacher Identity. *Teaching and Teacher Education*, 27(2): 308-19.

Canrinus, E, Helms-Lorenz, M, Beijaard, D, Buitink, J and Hofman, A (2012) Self-efficacy, Job Satisfaction, Motivation and Commitment: Exploring the Relationships between Indicators of Teachers' Professional Identity. *European Journal of Psychology of Education*, 27: 115-32.

Day, C, Kington, A, Stobart, G and Sammons, P (2006) The Personal and Professional Selves of Teachers: Stable and Unstable Identities. *British Educational Research Journal*, 32(4): 601-16.

Hart, R (2007) Act Like a Teacher: Teaching as a Performing Art. *Doctoral Dissertations*. [online] Available at: https://scholarworks.umass.edu/dissertations/AAI3275803/ (accessed 1 July 2022).

Howard, C, Carroll, J, Owens, J and Langston, D (2020) *The School Mentor's Guide: How to Mentor New and Beginning Teachers*. London: Learning Matters, Sage Publications.

Kornelsen, L (2006) Teaching with Presence. *New Directions for Adults and Continuing Education*, 111: 73-82.

Meijer, P, Korthagen, F and Vasalos, A (2009) Supporting Presence in Teacher Education: The Connection between the Personal and Professional Aspects of Teaching. *Teaching and Teacher Education*, 25(2): 297-308.

Nias, J (2014) Changing Times, Changing Identities: Grieving for a Lost Self. In Burgess, R G (ed) *Educational Research and Evaluation for Policy and Practice* (pp 139-56). London: Routledge.

O'Connor, K (2008) 'You Choose to Care': Teachers, Emotions and Professional Identity. *Teaching and Teacher Education*, 25(2): 297-308.

Paige, R, Geeson, R and Lambert, S (2020) *Building Skills for Effective Primary Teaching*. London: Learning Matters, Sage Publications.

Palombo, M and Daly, C (2021) *Mentoring Geography Teachers in the Secondary School: A Practical Guide*. London: Routledge.

Chapter 2   The need for professional development

What? (The big idea)

Continued professional development

No matter what you encounter when training, or the professional experiences you have had so far, your first class and year of teaching will prove to be a memorable, exciting but steep learning curve. Therefore, being an ECT should be seen rather as the next stage of your development, providing a bridge between your identity as a trainee teacher and feeling like an experienced professional. Not only will you be establishing your sense of who you are professionally (as outlined in Chapter 1), ie your professional identity, but you will also be striving to build upon what you have learned so far to be the best teacher you can be. Remember, no one will expect you to know everything when you first start your teaching career. However, it is important that you get the support and guidance you need in order to thrive. As the *Early Career Framework* (ECF) (DfE, 2019, p 24) notes, your professional development *'is likely to be sustained over time, involve expert support or coaching and opportunities for collaboration'*. It will be integral to your induction to the profession and the school in which you have chosen to teach. As the Department for Education (2021) outlines, this induction period will help you meet your professional development needs. This will be achieved by an agreed programme of training which will help you understand and apply the knowledge and skills set out by the ECF. For many teachers, training or professional development is sometimes referred to as continuing professional development (CPD), a term which seems worthy given your learning will never stop. As Spencer et al (2017, p 35) indicate, your professional development is likely to take the form of what they see as '*mixed provision*', including both informal and formal methods. No matter where you are in your career, everyone needs to learn in order to grow personally and professionally. Professional development therefore can be seen as an ongoing process and considered as learning to help you build on the knowledge, skills and attitudes you already possess.

Informal professional development

Informal professional development is focused around opportunities for you to engage with your school-based colleagues and is centred around your class-based practice. Though every culture and setting will be different, support will be there for you in many different guises. This may include:

» other teachers in the school;

» your mentor;

» your induction mentor;

» subject co-ordinator;

» Special Educational Needs and Disabilities Co-ordinator (SENDCo);

» designated safeguarding lead (DSL);

» phase leads and senior leaders.

It may also extend to other colleagues outside your immediate setting who can guide you with advice and feedback, for example other ECT colleagues. Such informal means of professional development will allow you to gain timely, easily accessible and invaluable professional advice. Examples of support may be, for example, linked to support with planning a topic or advice regarding aspects of behaviour management linked to whole school policy.

Informal observations of your practice (these may also be complemented by scheduled, formalised observations of your teaching) will take place at regular intervals during your time as an ECT. This will enable your colleagues to support you, and to provide a fair and effective assessment of your progress and practice while also signalling to you the value you have in the school community. Informal feedback by your mentor (and/or induction tutor) or established teaching colleagues may also form the focus of your reflective practice (Howard et al, 2020). It may allow you to review what you are doing, give you confidence in your abilities and allow for the development of your self-efficacy. Remember the concept of reflective practice will not be new to you as an ECT. As part of your ITT you will have come across various models for reflection such as Schön (1991) and Brookfield (1995). You will have realised the benefits this may have for you professionally in terms of, for example, promoting a professional dialogue around your practice and/or helping you consider enhanced alternative models of practice which may or may not suit you and your professional approach. As Tarrant (2013) indicates, as someone new to the profession, your reflective practice does not now centre around passing a course; the best reflection will be centred around your own self-motivation in order to understand and to develop. It should be 'about learning and having a disposition to learn continuously' (Tarrant, 2013, p 13). Such a desire to develop and learn professionally may be assisted by engaging with new government advice, for example with approaches to teaching and learning and established/newly produced educational research. Though time will be precious, do try to keep abreast of this form of learning as part of enhancing your own professional development. Subject-specific or more general publications, such as *Primary Science* and the Education Endowment Foundation (EEF) website, can give you valuable insights into ideas and current educational thinking while also being an easily accessible read. Some schools subscribe to educational and subject-specific publications, and they may form the basis of a discussion point in the staffroom. In addition to this, staff meetings may also provide a means where colleagues might engage in sharing their views and reflections on teaching and learning. These may be linked to their professional experiences or from learning experiences they have recently engaged in. Also, if you find yourself employed in a school which forms part of a multi-academy trust (MAT) you may find you are able to join a 'research group' set up in such settings. These will enable you and other teachers to explore an educational research focus which may be pertinent to you, your setting and its practice or a wider professional matter which may enhance teaching and learning.

Formal professional development

More formal methods of CPD may complement and support your ongoing professional development. As an ECT, the ECF will support you with an entitlement to a fully funded, two-year package of structured training based around the best in available research. Such support for enhancing your teaching and your pupils' learning should be identified by you in collaboration with your induction tutor/mentor. More structured training might take the form of a package of courses delivered by your locally designated provider or wider forms of non-accredited training developed off site, for example the use of a literacy-based scheme. Over the course of the two years as an ECT you will hopefully have the opportunity to attend courses which will lead to your future accreditation – for example, a Mental Health First Aid or Paediatric First Aid course. Some additional formal training might be incorporated into dedicated professional development days or staff meetings, perhaps linked to new government initiatives, or when staff provide feedback to you on training they have attended (cascade training), or a particular whole school need. Such days may be led by your headteacher, other staff or outside agencies/organisations and may include other schools and their staff. These training opportunities may be linked to your wider academy or local cluster of schools.

Both formal or informal CPD will enhance you professionally and on a personal level. You should not see your professional development needs in terms of a personal shortcoming or a deficit in your abilities (Spencer et al, 2017). As authors such as Wenger (2000) indicate, we are part of a social learning community with others: a community of practice (Wenger, 1998). For some schools, the notion of professional development may include both ECT and more experienced teachers working together on a formalised developmental focus and even reporting their findings in relevant publications to share and disseminate good practice.

So what? ◀◀◀

Why is it interesting?

Professional development will serve to challenge your thinking as well as allowing you to reflect on your own strengths and weaknesses and the progress you have made. It will allow you to identify your next steps for further improvement to benefit both you and pupil learning outcomes.

Professional development will impact on your knowledge, skills and understanding as a teacher on many differing levels. As Stoll et al (2012, p 4) outline, this may be in in relation to your:

» personal capacity;

» practice;

» interpersonal capacity.

Personal capacity and practice

Engaging in future learning through professional development allows you to grow in a personal capacity in terms of your pedagogy and subject knowledge. It may also help you develop the skills needed to be a successful teacher as well as increasing your levels of motivation and self-confidence. It will allow you to consider and try out changes in your practice, and to see things from a new perspective, which can provide you with much-needed opportunities to reflect on what you have seen, what you have done and how you have done it.

Pedagogy and subject knowledge alongside constructive feedback will allow you to develop and experiment with new strategies and approaches to your class-based practice. By engaging with professional development your subject knowledge over time will be enhanced by specialised training, for example in the use of newly acquired schemes. Also, when you meet a new topic, for example teaching about the First World War, professional development may mean engaging with additional learning to build up a resource bank to teach such a topic effectively. This might involve web-based searches, exploring history schemes or liaising with a peer.

Interpersonal capacity and practice

As your career develops you will learn from others, and by them sharing their best practice and knowledge with you, you can become part of an effective team. Developing interpersonal skills and relationships with your peers allows you to know who to ask for advice and where to find it. As an ECT, time is precious, and by building personal relationships and an understanding of others' strengths you can quickly secure the help you need.

Reflective task ◀◀◀

Read the two case studies below and consider the importance and impact of professional support for the personal and professional development of these ECTs. Using the prompts after each case study, reflect upon the need for and impact of the outlined professional development.

Case study ◀◀◀

Sunil

Sunil has been teaching Year 4 in a small, mixed-aged primary school for nine months. He has recently had a looked-after child join his class and is feeling uncertain about how best to support him.

After an initial induction period in Sunil's class things started well for this child. However, as time has gone on it has become evident to Sunil that the behaviours the child is exhibiting are unfamiliar to him. These behaviours seem linked to this new child's previous life, home background and his move to being fostered. This is the first looked-after child Sunil's school has had in many years. Sunil has talked to his mentor to say that he is feeling out of his depth. Sunil's feelings derive from issues relating to this child's history and out of a desire to better understand how he can support this new child to succeed. Since there does not seem to be a local, timely course available for him, the mentor agrees for Sunil to visit a larger local cluster school who has had looked-after children over successive years and have supported fostered children.

By visiting the identified setting Sunil was given the chance to watch an experienced teacher support a looked-after child in his class and he was able to hear and see what strategies were being employed with this child. Sunil could also talk to the headteacher as the key liaison with the social worker and as someone who is responsible for the looked-after provision in the school. This professional development allowed Sunil to learn and consider what is important for the child, for example:

- a strong home liaison and transition from home to school. This helped the teacher know if the child is likely to bring into school issues carried over from being at home the night before;

- for any behavioural issues, the need to have consistent and clear boundaries to pre-empt any issues, for example linked to a contact visit, around the child's appreciation of personal space and the need for appropriate touching;

- a need to reduce anxiety by giving the child warning of changes in routine and to provide a visual timetable to reduce the child's confusion or need to retain information.

As a result of this visit Sunil was allowed much-needed training to support his practice. Though this development was informal in its nature, it allowed Sunil future access to a colleague whom Sunil could ask for advice and support. Sunil went back to his classroom having reflected on what he had seen relating to this focus. Sunil considered which strategies and ideas he could now integrate into his day-to-day practice to support his new child. As a result of this Sunil's actions included setting up a home-school book, implementing a visual timetable and using opportunities, such as before the child enters school, to warn his pupil of changes to his normal routine. Sunil also implemented the modelling for the child on how to respect other children's personal space.

Reflective task ◀◀◀

- What triggered Sunil's need to engage with professional development?

- How did Sunil seek advice for his professional need?

- Was Sunil's support through a formal or informal means of professional development? Why was such a route chosen?

- What were the benefits to Sunil's pedagogy and practice as a result of his professional development?

Case study ◀◀◀

Catherine

Catherine has been teaching Year 1 in an urban, two-form entry school for 18 months. Catherine was approached by her mentor and headteacher who asked her if she would be interested in helping to support the development of mental health and well-being in the school, with a view ultimately in the future of being the school's ambassador in this area. Pupils' mental health and well-being was a real passion for Catherine. She was excited to be asked to take on this work and to have the opportunity to develop her knowledge around this topic. This would involve her attending a Mental Health First Aid course to support her personal and professional knowledge. This took place for a couple of days outside her setting at a designated training centre with many other professionals being present. Catherine learned about topics such as the range of mental health and well-being conditions, how to spot the warning signs and symptoms, how to reduce the stigma around mental health and how to support mental health in the workplace.

As a result of the course Catherine had an enhanced knowledge relating to the mental health and well-being of children and adults. The course had given her the confidence to help support other colleagues and she felt she was now able to signpost them to areas of support. Catherine, alongside the SENDCo, reviewed the school policy relating to mental health and well-being, adding aspects of her new knowledge and ideas gleaned from her tutors and other school colleagues who attended the course. Both Catherine and the SENDCo reviewed the numerous strategies the school had in place currently to support pupils' and staff's mental health and well-being. This also meant Catherine could also suggest ideas gleaned from talking to other teachers in various settings that might benefit her school.

Reflective task ◀◀◀

- What triggered Catherine to engage with professional development?

- Was Catherine's support through a formal or informal means of professional development? Why was such a route chosen?

- What were the benefits to Catherine's pedagogy and practice as a result of her professional development?

- Did Catherine's professional development have a wider professional impact for her? If so, what?

Reflective task ◀◀◀

Thinking about your own professional development, consider the value of professional development to you with regard to your pedagogy and practice. How does it impact upon you both personally and professionally? Use the questions below as a prompt for your reflections on this notion.

- What triggers lead you to seeking professional development?

  Top tip: By continually reflecting on your practice and being honest with yourself you will quickly be able to identify where and when professional development is needed.

- How do you make professional development timely?

  Top tip: If you feel you need support, seek help as soon as possible, rather than waiting. Such a delay may affect you personally and your professional abilities.

- What factors might affect where you can gain support?

  Top tip: Remember, there may not always be a designated course available that can support your immediate need. Professional development can sometimes be best provided by other experienced professionals in similar settings.

- What is the impact to you of the professional development?

  Top tip: By attending a professional development event it will give you time to reflect upon your current practice, enhance your motivation and confidence as well as giving you additional pedagogical and subject knowledge.

- Do you think professional development has a long-lasting professional impact? If so, why?

Top tip: As a teacher we are like magpies picking up nuggets of gold, using them and storing them. Sometimes you will not always see the immediate impact, but over time things learned in professional development will fit into place and be useful to you.

Now what?

Looking forward

Whether you are at the start of your journey as an ECT or a more long-serving experienced teacher, professional development forms the bedrock on which effective practice is built. Having left full-time education you may now be feeling that you do not wish to engage in any more courses or learning – however, this will change. As your career starts, you will engage in professional development either out of necessity or curiosity. Learning is infectious and your desire to understand and be the best will drive the need for future learning. As Chapter 1 suggested, reflexive practice is a professional skill that is needed by you as a developing teacher and for you to become adaptable. By reflecting continually on your professional self you will be able to identify your strengths and areas for development. Professional development will be supported by your induction and ongoing discussion and reviews with your mentor. Some of these developmental needs will be immediate in order for you to survive and thrive; others may emerge as you meet new and challenging situations. By sharing your journey with others you will be able to map out your future course of learning. Such a route map will instil in you the skills, knowledge and attitudes to become a success.

The practical tasks suggested below are a starting point for your ongoing professional development.

Practical task for tomorrow ◀◀◀

Consider your most immediate strengths and concerns regarding your own professional development. Using the template provided (Table 2.1), put a shortlist together to identify what you would like to achieve over time.

Table 2.1 Professional audit

Professional audit		
Strengths		
Knowledge	**Skills and attitudes**	**Timescale**
Detailed knowledge of phonics and its usage in class.	*Good at communicating with my colleagues and parents.*	Currently
Areas for development		
Promoting challenge in my teaching of the most able of pupils.		Currently
	Report writing	Spring term

Practical task for next week ◀◀◀

Talk to your mentor and headteacher about the year ahead. Use your list from the task above as a starting point. Explore with them what expert support, coaching and opportunities for collaboration and courses are available to suit your identified developmental needs.

Practical task for the long term ◀◀◀

At the end of your first year at school revisit with your mentor and headteacher what your future professional development needs are. Examine, with them, how your professional development can contribute to whole school needs and development.

What next? ◀◀◀

This chapter has explored with you the importance of professional development as an ECT. Throughout the chapter a key message is that professional development can be gained by both formal and informal methods. As a result of this input, you can develop professionally in terms of your pedagogical knowledge and skills. You may also find that when your developmental needs are met you can be enhanced personally in terms of, for example, your attitude and confidence with teaching or dealing with situations. Professional development will also help you develop your identity as a teacher. It will help ensure that you are progressing forward as you develop a sense of who you are as a teacher. Remember, as an ECT you will now be on a lifelong journey of learning; professional development will prove the bedrock of future success for you and all your colleagues.

Further reading

Chartered College of Teaching (2020) *The Early Career Framework Handbook*. London: Sage Publications.

Evans, L (1998) *Teacher Morale, Job Satisfaction and Motivation*. London: Cassells.

Jones, K and MacPherson, R (2021) *The Teaching Life: Professional Learning and Career Progression*. Woodbridge: John Catt Educational.

References

Brookfield, S (1995) *Becoming a Critically Reflective Teacher*. San Francisco, CA: Jossey-Bass.

Department for Education (DfE) (2019) *Early Career Framework.* [online] Available at: https://assets.publishing.service.gov.uk/government/uploads/system/uploads/attachment_data/file/978358/Early-Career_Framework_April_2021.pdf (accessed 1 July 2022).

Department for Education (DfE) (2021) *Induction for Early Career Teachers (England)*. [online] Available at: https://assets.publishing.service.gov.uk/government/uploads/system/uploads/attachment_data/file/972316/Statutory_Induction_Guidance_2021_final__002_____1___1_.pdf (accessed 1 July 2022).

Howard, C, Carroll, J, Owens, J and Langston, D (2020) *The School Mentor's Guide: How to Mentor New and Beginning Teachers.* London: Learning Matters, Sage Publications.

Schön, D (1991) *The Reflective Practitioner: How Professionals Think and Act.* Oxford: Avebury.

Spencer, P, Harrop, S, Thomas, J and Cain, T (2017) The Professional Development Needs of Early Career Teachers, and the Extent to Which They Are Met: A Survey of Teachers in England. *Professional Development in Education*, 44(1): 33–46.

Stoll, L, Harris, A and Handscomb, G (2012) *Great Professional Development Which Leads to Great Pedagogy: Nine Claims from Research.* [online] Available at: https://assets.publishing.service.gov.uk/government/uploads/system/uploads/attachment_data/file/335707/Great-professional-development-which-leads-to-great-pedagogy-nine-claims-from-research.pdf (accessed 20 July 2022).

Tarrant, P (2013) *Reflective Practice and Professional Development*. London: Sage.

Wenger, E (1998) *Communities of Practice: Learning, Meaning and Identity*. Cambridge: Cambridge University Press.

Wenger, E (2000) Communities of Practice and Social Learning Systems. *Organization*, 7(2): 225–46.

Chapter 3   Who can help me be a better teacher?

What? (The big idea) ◀ ◀ ◀

Why others?

As an ECT, the initial period of your career can sometimes feel daunting, given the range of your professional responsibilities. However, you are never alone; there will be many colleagues sharing this journey and they can help and support you to grow and flourish. You are now part of a whole school culture whose mission it is to keep children safe and to develop the 'whole child'. Relationships with others can help you enhance the quality of your teaching, provide you with emotional support and promote excellence in your practice. Colleagues may also give you general, specialist and additional support for the children in your care. This may include identified professionals such as the SENDCo and teaching assistants (TA). These ongoing relationships with others can foster a shared responsibility for enhancing children's lives. As an ECT, the DSL will be there to support you should you have any safeguarding concerns. As publications such as that by the Department for Education (2021, p 7) rightly point out, '*safeguarding and promoting the welfare of children is everyone's responsibility'*. As an ECT, safeguarding can be a very daunting aspect of your new career. Remember, this duty is something you should not carry on your own. Your responsibility will mainly lie with being vigilant for any concerns, reporting them and knowing who to contact if you have concerns. Alongside working with your colleagues, effective relationships with parents will be of paramount importance to your success, enabling you to work together to support and enhance children's well-being and academic progress. This chapter helps to explore the need to establish this myriad of relationships in order to keep children safe, to secure their progress and to promote your future success.

Who can you turn to?

Teaching is not a solitary profession and developing positive relationships with others will enable you to draw on the experience and expertise of others to support you to make a valuable contribution to the wider life of your school and its culture of success. Teamwork is vital if you are to ease successfully into your new profession. As Huberman (1993, p 43) suggests, you can experience a *'painful beginning'* or an *'easy beginning'* to your career, attributing a *'painful beginning'* to teachers who are remote from their peers and an *'easy beginning'* where teachers have a working bond with their colleagues. Such *'collaboration'* (Brunetti and Marston, 2018, p 880), ie, working with others, can involve the *'informal exchange of ideas or materials to deliberate planning and joint implementation of new curricula'*. As they suggest, for those teachers new to their careers it may also involve asking for advice which can enable them to deal with the daily stresses of class-based practice. Spicksley and Watkins (2020) note that informal relationships with colleagues are formed organically, and that such connections are open and involve trusting conversations with their peers. These relationships can be seen to have a positive impact on teachers' resilience and commitment (Spicksley and Watkins, 2020), to be a means of shaping their identity and, in some cases, to create a heightened sense of agency (Brunetti and Marston, 2018).

Alongside working and gaining support from your general colleagues, your practice will also involve working in more formal ways with identified professionals in your school. One such individual, who can provide much invaluable support, is your mentor: an individual you can trust, who can help you to reflect upon your practice and is able to help you achieve your future professional aspirations (Howard et al, 2020). There will also be several other key professionals, as well as year group leads and subject leads, with whom you will need to engage if you are to secure the best of practice. This will include your SENDCo, TA and/or DSL.

SENDCo

You will have a diverse range of needs and challenges in your classroom and therefore all children will progress at different rates socially, emotionally and academically. With pupils who need additional support with their progress, you will, as the Special Educational Needs and Disability Code of Practice states (DfE, 2015, p 95), support them with '*high-quality teaching targeted at their areas of weakness*'. Where progress continues to be less than expected you will need to work with the SENDCo to ascertain if special educational needs (SEN) support is needed. The SENDCo is one of the professionals you can turn to in order to enhance your ability to deliver targeted learning to identified children in your care. SENDCos, as the Department for Education (2015) indicates, are able to co-ordinate the detailed provision of pupils with SEN and those with an Education, Health and Care (EHC) plan in schools.

As well as being a source of help and support, the SENDCo can help you support pupils with additional needs through a graduated approach (which involves a cycle of Assess, Plan, Do and Review; DfE, 2015). Part of this process will involve liaising with and working closely with other professionals (for example, educational psychologists as part of multi-agency working). Your SENDCo will be able to provide you with suitable interventions that may help in your day-to-day practice to support pupils with additional needs. Such interventions may be for academic, social or emotional needs and may be delivered through you and/or your TA. This can take place in class or via identified interventions outside of lessons with focused teaching. Remember that SEN present in many different ways. For some pupils, your teaching, alongside identified interventions, may only result in small incremental gains. However, any such small gains may indicate great success for some individuals. By working in partnership with your SENDCo you will make a difference to the lives and futures of the children you teach.

Reflective task ◀◀◀

How confident are you that you know what the SEND Code of Practice says with regard to identifying and supporting various needs in schools? Read Chapter 6 ('Identifying SEN in schools') in the SEND Code of Practice (DfE, 2015). Reflect and record your responses to the following questions.

- What are the four broad areas of need?

- Have you seen examples of these in your practice so far?

- What four-part cycle do interventions go through?

- What additional services can SENDCos/schools call upon to assess and support children's needs?

Teaching assistants

For those teachers who are fortunate to have a TA or a member of support staff, they may prove to be one of the most significant adults in your professional life. In some schools, a TA may be with you at all times; in others, they may support in your classroom as one part of a much wider role. You will find that the professional relationship you develop with your TA will be key if you are to have a strong and productive working partnership. Research such as Mackenzie (2011, p 65) indicate that TAs *'very often have a strong commitment to work and an emotional connection to the people they work with'*. As this research notes, TAs will invest time in you and your classroom. If you get this relationship right, they can become an invaluable additional pair of eyes and ears for you in the classroom, not only to help and inform pupils' assessments but also to let you know of any possible safeguarding issues. TAs can be much-valued colleagues and sounding boards. As the EEF (2013, p 7) indicates, TAs can free up teachers from some of their classroom responsibilities such as preparing and organising resources in order to *'focus more time on the core functions of teaching – such as planning, assessment and time spent in class'*.

The way you approach working with your TA will be fundamental to your relationship with them. Given, as Hayes (2003, p 9) notes, *'many assistants give their time over and above their hours'*, it is important that your rapport with your TA is built on mutual respect and not taking *'what they do for granted'*. Negotiating a productive working relationship with your TA can be daunting when joining a school, but it is worth investing time and energy into doing so. The knowledge they possess about your children, families and how the school works can be an invaluable source of information. This can inform and support your practice and help you become a better teacher.

To support your practice and to provide an effective learning environment, it is important to utilise the many talents that a TA possesses. For example, if they particularly enjoy cooking, this ability can feed into your planning and be utilised when undertaking a topic or numeracy activity.

One barrier that can often exist when sustaining an effective relationship with your TA is finding time to communicate with them. This is primarily due to their working with children in lesson time and sometimes having to go (at the end of the lesson) to support another class or take on another role. As the EEF (2013, p 9) suggests, *'communication between teachers and TAs is largely ad hoc'*, with TAs *'feeling underprepared for the tasks they are given'*. However, as Goddard and Ryall (2002) indicate, it is vital for the understanding of the benefit and efficacy of planning and tasks that time is given over for teachers to discuss teaching and learning with their TA. This sharing of planned lesson outcomes is considered vital within the *Early Career Framework* (DfE, 2019). If TAs are to understand their role in lessons and know what is required of them, communication is going to be key. Some teachers overcome limited discussion times, for example, by leaving communication notes or recording comments in a communication book. Everyone will be different. It will be up to you to find what works best for you and your TA.

The deployment of your TA will be essential if you wish to be as effective as possible in your promotion of teaching and learning. Unfortunately, as the EEF (2013) notes, the support for pupils by TAs is often centred around lower-attaining pupils, is informal and instructional in its nature, is directed at task completion and is less focused on children developing understanding. Therefore, as the *Early Career Framework* (DfE, 2019) rightly sets out, make certain that your TA is providing extra support and is not used as a replacement for the teacher.

Reflective task ◀◀◀

- Find a sheet of A3 paper and draw an image of yourself in the middle.

- Next use some sticky notes to write down what tasks your TA currently undertakes to support you and your practice.

- Place the sticky notes on the paper, with those which have the most impact on your professional development, or the learning of children, closest to the centre and those with less impact further away.

- Use the EEF (2018) document *Making Best Use of Teaching Assistants, Summary of Recommendations* to reflect upon your own current practice with your TA that is now displayed around the image of yourself.

- In light of this, consider whether you need any of these roles to be changed or amended.

Top tips ◀◀◀

- Consider rotating your TA around all of your attaining groups so they have a range of experiences supporting pupils.

- It is important you give your TA a role beyond that of supporting pupils in groups. Give them opportunities to raise their status when they are with you, eg modelling a concept to the whole class/contributing to whole class teaching.

- By giving TAs the same intervention to carry out year on year they will begin to know it well. They can then tailor their resources so they are most effective for them when supporting children.

Parents and carers

As Goepel et al (2015) indicate, not only will parents and carers know their child best but they will have established the most effective means to support and help them with the barriers they face in life. As such, they can offer advice and information that will be invaluable. For example, if a child is not sleeping very well, it may be affecting their mood in class. Given this knowledge, you could arrange to work with the parent or carer to find a solution to support a more structured bedtime.

Some parents and carers can find interacting with teachers and a school setting a daunting experience. If this is the case, you will need to place them at their ease to promote a positive, working partnership with you. Communication will also be key to make the most of your engagement with parents and carers, involving them in their child's education. Liaising and talking to individuals can either take place informally, such as at the end of the day when dismissing children, or more formally through events such as parents' evening. Such means of dialogue are really important to discuss pupil progress and any concerns you or they may have. However, there may be some discussions where more time is needed. If this is the case, arrange for a specific meeting to be set up and, where necessary, involve other professionals such as the SENDCo. They will be able to offer you help, advice or support to get the best out of the meeting. Time will be precious in whatever meeting you are involved in so be prepared with what you wish to discuss and have the necessary information available at hand. Remember, positive relationships and effective communication with parents and carers will also be necessary should any safeguarding arise.

Reflective task ◀◀◀

Use the following questions to reflect upon your current working relationships with parents and carers.

- What opportunities do you have to liaise and discuss their child's progress?

- Consider what 'education speak' might you use that may not be easily understood, eg Standard Attainment Tests (SATs).

- How can you promote access to individuals who may be reluctant to talk to you?

Top tips ◀◀◀

- Never talk to parents and carers about their child in a social setting with others present. Individuals might appear to be happy for you to talk when friends are around but their child's education should remain confidential.

- Even simple terms such as attainment and progress may be difficult for some parents to understand; gauge your language so it is audience appropriate.

- If individuals are reluctant to engage with you, find positive, creative means to engage with them. For example, send a child out at the end of the day with a photocopy of their work and invite their parent(s)/carer(s) in to talk to you about it, or make a quick phone call home to praise a pupil's effort, attendance or attitude in class. This can form a bridge between you and parents/carers.

So what? ◀ ◀ ◀

Why is it interesting?

By building strong close working relationships with your colleagues, you will become part of a mutually supportive school environment, part of a culture that promotes a shared responsibility for improving the lives of all its pupils and a place where children feel safe. Effective relationships can serve to enhance your job satisfaction by enabling you to feel more confident and competent in what you do, thus enabling you to become a better teacher as well as helping to improve pupils' motivation, behaviour and academic success.

Seeking help and advice from a range of your peers will allow you to tap into a depth and breadth of professional knowledge. This will not only enhance your day-to-day class-based practice but will bring you a rich mine of professional expertise. Remember, no one should work on their own. Having good relationships with your professional colleagues should be fun, enjoyable and also professionally informative.

Professional relationships, whether they be with your mentor, colleagues or parents, will be underpinned by effective communication, trust and empathy. They will help you best support and overcome the challenges many pupils face, whether they be social, emotional or academic. Professional relationships with named individuals can advise and signpost you to the best means possible to support children and advise how to keep them safe. Strong working relationships with your TA and parents/carers can also help you form a more holistic picture of a child, with your understanding enhanced by the additional perspectives other adults can provide.

Reflective task ◀◀◀

Read Maksym's case study. Maksym is in his second term of his ECT first year. Consider the importance and impact that other professionals and liaising with parents/carers can have on the teaching and learning of one of his pupils. Then use the prompts after the case study to reflect on how you can be a better teacher as a result of working with others.

Case study ◀◀◀

Maksym

Maksym's pupil, Suzanne, recently had caused him more and more concerns. She had been in his Year 1 class for about a term and had started to fall behind her peers with her reading. Her writing showed common spelling errors, words that used reversals of letters such as 'b' and 'd' and she had limited use of punctuation. Suzanne found the pace of lessons difficult. Since she moved up from Reception, Suzanne's understanding of lessons had been hampered by her limited vocabulary. Maksym has not been made aware of any additional needs Suzanne had from the previous class teacher. The previous class teacher thought any limitations with her reading and writing might be linked to her summer birthday. To support Suzanne, Maksym had provided high-quality support in his classroom by, for example, giving her word banks to support her writing. Maksym had also moved Suzanne closer to the front of the classroom so she was nearer to him. Maksym made certain Suzanne was heard reading daily to try and maintain her reading level and that her book was regularly changed. Suzanne was reluctant to take her book home and often left her book behind in class when going home. Maksym had also asked the TA to check in with Suzanne. Maksym had started to share his concerns with her parents at the last parents' evening.

As a result of Maksym's concerns he talked to the SENDCo (Laura). Laura had suggested she come and spend some time in class to observe Suzanne and to look at the quality of her work. As a result of this Laura and Maksym both talked to the parents about their growing concerns. After this, it was agreed that Laura would undertake some initial screening tests with Suzanne for any issues around dyslexia. Following this and another meeting with the parents, Laura agreed to place Suzanne on the SEND school register. These steps allowed Laura to request some more detailed assessments of Suzanne's challenges and to be able to investigate what other strategies could be best put in place to support Suzanne's needs.

Reflective task ◀◀◀

Use the questions below as a prompt for your reflections on Maksym's story and his engagement with his SENDCo.

• What triggered Maksym's concerns?

Top tip: You continually need to be vigilant for the telltale signs that children are falling behind the rest of their peers. Talk to other colleagues and the teacher who had the pupils before you if you are uncertain about what to do.

• Do you think Maksym was right to talk to the SENDCo when he did? If yes, why?

Top tip: If you are worried about a pupil, have an informal talk to your SENDCo to sound them out regarding your concerns. Do not delay such conversations. Remember, SENDCos hold the bigger picture regarding pupil progress and will be able to use this to advise you.

• Why was it important they both talk to parents about Suzanne's progress now?

Top tip: You will need to take parents with you if you are going to progress down a SEND identification and placing on the register. You cannot act without their support unless it is a safeguarding issue.

• What might being on the SEND school register provide for Suzanne in the future?

Top tip: Timely communication with the SENDCo is important so that pupils can receive diagnostic testing, specialist support/strategies and resources to help support their needs as soon as practical.

Now what? ◀ ◀ ◀

Looking forward

Practical task for tomorrow ◀◀◀

Make a list of those professionals you have engaged with so far and how you have worked with them so as to make you a better teacher. Use this list as a basis for a conversation with other colleagues or your mentor. Discuss how engaging with those professionals has made you a better teacher.

Practical task for next week ◀◀◀

Observation task – with appropriate consent, arrange to observe another teacher engaging with a professional colleague or parent/carer. Consider how what you observed may benefit you personally and professionally. Jot down your reflections or record them using a template such as the one below in Table 3.1.

Table 3.1 Observational record

Professional	Point under discussion	Personal insights	Professional outcome
Eg SENDCo	Strategies used to manage challenging behaviours.	It enabled me to see that other teachers also need strategies such as time out of the situation to help calm down a child. Despite their experience they still need the support of a SENDCo.	I learned a range of strategies I was unaware of such as a home–school log and time out from the situation if things are not going well for the child.
Eg teaching assistant	To explore how the TA can set up a social intervention group.	I can see I need to agree with my TA when will be the best time to withdraw a group if they have an intervention.	New awareness of 'social speaking' style intervention and how it can be used to support children's social skill.
Eg parent	Concern for a pupil's reading	I can see it is important to share our own insights in the child's progress. Also, to understand the child and how the child is with their reading at home.	It is important to revisit concerns with a review meeting around progress and strategies in order to keep lines of communication open.

Practical task for the long term ◀◀◀

After you complete a full academic year, review the relationships you have formed with colleagues, parents/carers or other identified professionals. Consider: have you engaged with them weekly, monthly or rarely? What difference would it have made to your effectiveness if you had sought their help or support earlier? Create your own format or use Figure 3.1 to make a resolution which will help you be a more effective teacher as a result of liaising with parents/carers and professionals.

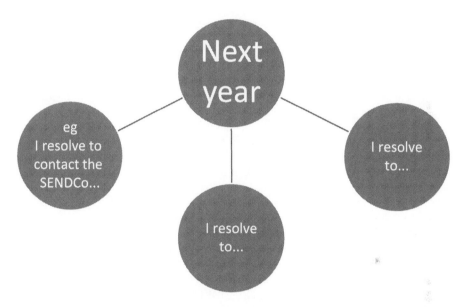

Figure 3.1 New academic year's resolutions

What next? ◀ ◀ ◀

This chapter has explored the importance of your colleagues, other designated professionals and parents and carers in developing your professional practice and in better understanding the children in your care. These relationships will support and enhance your knowledge of pupils, promote their learning and keep them safe. All of this will enable you to be a better teacher. Building a rapport with other adults will allow you to access advice and enhance your own professional knowledge. It may also give you the confidence and abilities necessary to deal with new and challenging situations.

Further reading

Devi, A (2020) *Essential Guides for Early Career Teachers: Special Educational Needs and Disability*. St Albans: Critical Publishing.

Freeman, C and Gates, J (2022) *We Need to Talk about Parents: A Teachers' Guide to Working with Families*. London: Corwin.

Webster, R, Russell, A and Blatchford, P (2015) *Maximising the Impact of Teacher Assistants. Guidance for School Leaders and Teachers*. 2nd ed. Abingdon: Routledge.

References

Brunetti, G J and Marston, S H (2018) A Trajectory of Teacher Development in Early and Mid-career. *Teachers and Teaching*, 24(8): 874–92.

Department for Education (DfE) (2015) *Special Educational Needs and Disability Code of Practice: 0 to 25 Years.* London: DfE.

Department for Education (DfE) (2019) *Early Career Framework*. [online] Available at: https://assets.publishing.service.gov.uk/government/uploads/system/uploads/attachment_data/file/978358/Early-Career_Framework_April_2021.pdf (accessed 1 July 2022).

Department for Education (DfE) (2021) *Keeping Children Safe in Education 2021. Statutory Guidance for Schools and Colleges*. [online] Available at: https://assets.publishing.service.gov.uk/government/uploads/system/uploads/attachment_data/file/1021914/KCSIE_2021_September_guidance.pdf (accessed 19 May 2022).

Education Endowment Foundation (EEF) (2013) *Making Best Use of Teaching Assistants. Guidance Report.* [online] Available at: https://maximisingtas.co.uk/assets/content/taguidancereportmakingbestuseofteachingassisstants.pdf (accessed 15 May 2022).

Education Endowment Foundation (EEF) (2018) *Making Best Use of Teaching Assistants. Summary of Recommendations*. [online] Available at: https://d2tic4wvo1iusb.cloudfront.net/eef-guidance-reports/teaching-assistants/TA_Recommendations_Summary.pdf?v=1635870535 (accessed 22 June 2022).

Goepel, J, Childerhouse, H and Sharpe, S (2015) *Inclusive Primary Teaching*. 2nd ed. Northwich: Critical Publishing.

Goddard, G and Ryall, A (2002) Teaching Assistants: Issues for the Primary School. *Primary Practice*, 3: 29–32.

Hayes, D (2003) *A Student Teacher's Guide to Primary School Placement: Learning to Survive and Prosper*. London: RoutledgeFalmer.

Howard, C, Carroll, J, Owens, J and Langston, D (2020) *The School Mentor's Guide: How to Mentor New and Beginning Teachers*. London: Learning Matters, Sage Publications.

Huberman, M (1993) *The Lives of Teachers*. London: Cassell.

Mackenzie, S (2011) 'Yes, But ...': Rhetoric, Reality and Resistance in Teaching Assistants' Experiences of Inclusive Education. *Support for Learning*, 26(2): 64–71.

Spicksley, K and Watkins, M (2020) Early-Career Teachers' Relationships with Peers and Mentors: Exploring Policy and Practice. In Kington, A and Blackmore, K (eds) *Social and Learning Relationships in Primary School* (pp 93–115). Oxford: Bloomsbury Academic.

Chapter 4   No one is an island: how can others help me become a better teacher?

What? (The big idea)

No one is an island

> *No man is an island entire of itself;*
> *every man is a piece of the continent,*
> *a part of the main*

Donne, 1988, lines 1–4

Do you know the poem by John Donne with the line '*No man is an island entire of itself*'? To summarise the essence of the poem: no one exists and works in isolation; they are part of something bigger, something stronger. The poem is an encouragement to be involved in your community and to recognise the strength of being part of something beyond yourself. Donne (1988) describes this as *'part of the continent ... part of the main'*, and this provides great imagery for understanding how communities and engagement in those communities can bring us strength and connection. In this chapter there is opportunity for you to consider your place within your school learning community, working with different people and how you can work in a reciprocal way to develop as an ECT in your school community. This chapter also helps you recognise how different types of relationships can bring opportunities for personal and professional development, as well as offering a support network which is so important in these early years of your teaching career.

Some people seem to be good at building a positive network of people around them who are motivated to help and encourage them so that they can be successful. They seem to draw people to them and have a disposition where they can 'fit' easily into the community. This is not always so easy for others and this chapter explores how you can develop trust and positive relationships, develop confidence to be able to ask for help and articulate what you need, as well as develop approaches so that you are open to feedback. For some of you in your ECT phase, it will support you in ensuring you are clear about how others can help you and why it is important to allow others to help, and to seek out that expertise in more experienced or more knowledgeable people. This chapter is not just about how the formal ECT mentoring can be enhanced, but how you as an ECT can work with trainers, mentors and teacher colleagues, parents and carers as well as senior leaders to build your network (Wilhelm et al, 2020).

Ubuntu: I am because we are

I recently learnt of a South African term, *'Ubuntu'* (Ogude, 2018). You may already be aware of this phrase, and you may even use it in your own vocabulary. I understand there are slight variations in its meaning, but a common understanding of the phrase is *'I am because we are'* (Ogude, 2018). In this concept is a sense of the relationships between people within the community, which will be fundamental to your school experiences, while also recognising how communities and groups can have an identity and culture of their own. Interestingly, the essence of this concept of Ubuntu challenges some of the ideas presented in Chapter 1 where the emphasis is on how you, as an individual, develop your own identity; this is a different way to think about your personhood (Ogude, 2018). It is a philosophy that your networks, your connections to others and your engagement with communities influence your identity and the way you are in the world. Ubuntu expresses the interpersonal aspects of compassion, caring and reciprocity (Ogude, 2018). We shall explore the idea of reciprocity further and how important the formal community (for example, your school) and the informal community (for example, the networks you create) are to you as you become a wonderful teacher.

Start to think about the different communities you participate in and how those people who make up those communities or groups influence the way you are in that context and how you view yourself (Ubuntu). If you would like to read more about Ubuntu and related education projects and topics, *The Elephant Times*, an online magazine, is a great resource (see further reading).

So what?

We start from the premise that you recognise how influential your communities and networks are upon you, and that they can influence how successful you are. Many social psychologists have explored aspects of group behaviour and how we are influenced, or persuaded, by the groups in which we engage (see, for example, Cialdini, 2007 and the exploration of 'social proof'). If we unpick this further, there are some key components for you to consider as you establish yourself as part of a supportive and enabling community that you can proactively encourage and manage. While you will not be able to control every aspect, for example who is assigned as your ECT mentor, you will be able to manage how you build extended networks, trust and reciprocal working, and your openness to feedback. These are some of the aspects we are going to delve deeper into so that you can make conscious and informed choices about the impact others have upon your successes. There are many resources around you; some will be offered through the formal arrangements during your ECT phase but others you can seek out and establish as part of your own development, and ownership of that development. As you read the following exploration of how others can help you in your ECT phase, keep in mind how communication needs to underpin these different aspects, and how important it is for you to be able to communicate clearly what you need. Mostly, you will find that people in your school community will want you to flourish and will want to help you become a brilliant teacher.

Formal and informal network building

As an ECT, some of the social capital you will gain will be through the networks that you establish (Fox and Wilson, 2015). These networks are constructed from a range of sources which go beyond the formal roles, such as ECT mentor. Social capital can be expressed simply as the benefits of developing relationships that are rooted in mutual respect and trust, so that ambitions and goals can be realised (Fox and Wilson, 2015). Some of our networks are established for us, especially the formal ones, as your mentor and senior leaders in the school will have been appointed externally to you. They have been recognised for their experience and expertise and it is helpful for you to consider how the skills that they have can support you. For example, your senior leadership team will have expertise in giving constructive feedback and you need to be open to that feedback (even if some feedback, at times, might be hard to hear) so that it will help you develop. Keep in mind that these people in your formal network within school have an interest in your success. Like the ideas above around Ubuntu: your success will also be their success. The wonderful things that you bring to the classroom will enhance the provision, quality and even reputation of the school. So, professionally those people forming your formal network, even if they are people you would not have personally chosen to be part of that formal network, will all want you to succeed from a professional standpoint.

It is a good point here to acknowledge the wider culture within education. While this principle may not be true for all, generally within education, there is an emphasis on collaboration in supporting each other and in sharing expertise. This makes education a positive field to work within and it is helpful to recognise this culture and ensure that you are contributing positively to that culture, too. This means that people in your formal network will not only want you to succeed because of their professional responsibilities and the roles they hold, but you will meet many people in education with a genuine desire to see you flourish on a personal level and will want to do all they can to support you.

This point leads to thinking about the more informal professional network that you create around you. If you have joined a large school, or a school that is part of an academy structure, then look beyond your own phase or people that you work with closely and notice people that could be part of your professional network. Take the time to build respectful and trusting relationships through working reciprocally with them. Although you are the ECT, there are things you can bring to the professional relationship and things that established teachers can learn from you, too. It can also be supportive as you build your network to keep in touch with people from your ITT provider, for example ITT mentors/tutors and your peers. Many providers appreciate keeping in touch with their ECTs and there are reciprocal ways for you to work with the next cohort of new teachers, while many ITT providers tutors will be happy to continue to support you. Using easily accessible ways to communicate and keep in touch, such as Twitter and LinkedIn, can mean that building this network is easier than you think. You will find a lot of support on Twitter, such as @MrTs_NQTs.

Both formal and informal networks need to be managed well; think about who you want in your informal network and how you will nurture those relationships. Reciprocal working builds trust and respect, which are key aspects of developing your social capital in your new working environment. In this next section, we start to think about some of the cornerstones of building meaningful networks: trust, connection and openness to feedback.

Building trust

The school context can be a complex place requiring negotiation and managed relationships. You will recognise from experience that building trust is a key part of any relationship and this is supported by several authors who identify trust as key in any professional context involving working with other people, such as within a school (see Bryk and Schneider, 2003, for example). There is an interesting idea by Steiha and Raider-Roth (2012) who explore the notion of a relational web in every school. This relational web acknowledges how different members of the school community interact, and the importance of the way that each of these people interact: through connection, relational trust and also, sometimes, disconnection.

Reflective task ◀◀◀

In the context of relational trust, and how trust is one of the components of a relational web, spend some time reflecting on the following questions.

Think about your own school environment and the formation of your own relational web.

- What part do you play and what things can you do in ensuring that relationships are built on trust (and connection)?

- How can you avoid negative situations that could lead to disconnection?

Trust is not something that just occurs; it is constructed and reinforced over time. Your new colleagues will begin to trust you as they witness your professional behaviours, such as ensuring you are punctual, well prepared and engaged in the school community, and as they get to see your work in action. You will gain credibility as colleagues see that you work hard to ensure that the learning opportunities for the pupils are as good as they can be, and also as they observe you striving for 'even better'. Simple actions such as recognising the contributions of other people, being grateful for the time and support others give to you as well as being a positive and pleasant character around school will all contribute to the trust your colleagues will have in you. Similarly, you will be looking for signs that you are able to trust colleagues and much of this comes through the experiences you have with colleagues. You will want to look around for those colleagues who have developed excellent classroom practice and who you can trust to give you helpful and supportive feedback – also, colleagues who have a collaborative and positive attitude which will enable opportunities for reciprocal working. Start to think about how you will demonstrate that you are a colleague who can be trusted in your school environment and how you can build that credibility quickly with your colleagues so that they respect your work in the school and know that your contributions will be positive and helpful.

Nurturing connection

As you contemplate your relational web in your school context, begin to think about how connection with others is created to support the development of your network. There will be some people that you find easy to work with and you feel comfortable with quite quickly. This can sometimes be based upon hierarchy and feeling that you are able to be increasingly open with people who are in a similar situation to you rather than someone who is, for example, a member of the senior leadership team (SLT). Similarly, you will have had experiences in your life when you have just connected with someone, and it is difficult to really understand why that connection occurred so easily. It may be that you have something in common, perhaps similar beliefs or values. Maybe you have a similar sense of humour or a similar taste in music or fashion or sport etc. However, you may have experienced a time when there is not a 'something in common' that connects you to the other person; the connection has been more about how you have supported each other. Helpfully, Miller and Stiver (1997) offer a way to think about this connection in relationships as mutual empathy for each other and that interactions are mutually empowering for all parties. This definition can be helpful to you in assessing the positive relationships in your varying networks and ensuring that there is reciprocity in those interactions. The mutual nature of this description aligns well with the idea of reciprocity that has been presented in this chapter. So, while you may consider that as an ECT you are the person receiving support and feedback and that you may not have much to offer more established colleagues, take some time to think carefully about what you can offer. Some ideas include working on projects together, sharing planning and resources, and helping to organise a school event. You will have lots more ideas specific to your context and the people with whom you work.

Openness

Building connections is a great skill to have and involves just the right amount of 'give and take'. This can be thought about as an energy (Rodenburg, 2007) where you are interested, positive and engaged in other people's work and you accept other people's interest and involvement in what you are doing, too. This leads on well to the idea of openness, which is an important professional attitude to adopt. You have joined a profession where feedback and areas for development are part of the culture: it would be rare to be observed and have no areas for development in education. Sometimes, receiving feedback on your teaching or around your professional role can feel extremely personal and you may feel defensive or uncomfortable in hearing an appraisal from a more experienced colleague. Consider your approach to receiving feedback: do you hear the positive aspects, or do you focus upon the negative or areas for development? Does your body language demonstrate an open attitude, and do you seek out feedback?

Reflective task ◀◀◀

You are going to create a visual representation of your professional network to help you to think about how those around you can support your ongoing professional development and help you to flourish.

- Start by thinking about those people who have the biggest influence on your professional development and support you in flourishing as a teacher. Think beyond just those who give you formal feedback and think about those who engage positively with you around professional dialogue or offer information that will help you support pupils in their learning.

- Place your name in the middle of a piece of paper and then write the names and roles of those with whom you have the most contact closest to your name. You will start to create a representation of how wide the scope of those who influence you are. Some of these people might be:

  - TAs;

  - ECT mentors;

  - phase leaders;

  - other ECTs (at your school or at other schools);

  - teachers in your phase;

  - parents/carers;

  - senior leaders;

  - school governors;

  - experts beyond your school (perhaps on social networks or from your training provider).

- Now take a different coloured pen and circle those who have the biggest impact on your career and opportunities. This is probably going to be the senior leaders in school, but it might be that there are other influential people in your school community, such as the school governors.

- Now take a different coloured pen again and identify those who have the most positive impact on your professional development.

- Have a look at your visual representation and think about how your network is supporting you in becoming the best teacher you can be. Do you need to draw upon more of the positive influences? Do you need to find a way to strengthen opportunities for those with the most influence and impact on your career?

There can be isolating experiences being an ECT (Shuck et al, 2017) and a sense of continuous scrutiny. The case study below describes the experience of Reggie, an ECT who was finding it initially challenging to build his supportive networks. With help from a trusted colleague, he was able to find approaches that enabled his success.

Case study ◀◀◀

Reggie has been working in a large primary school for a term. He has returned after the Christmas break feeling a little negative about school life. He is enjoying being with his class and he has developed good relationships with the children. However, the pace of school life and the requests from SLT and his ECT mentor have made him feel like he is not making progress or getting on top of the work expected of him. It seems like he always has actions to undertake, and that observation feedback does not recognise his hard work. Reggie has not expressed these feelings to his ECT mentor, but the feelings are causing him to feel unhappy and sometimes anxious, especially on a Sunday evening.

It is recognised that the ECT phase is a time of significant learning and that sometimes the amount of learning can feel overwhelming. It was really important that Reggie recognised the feelings he was experiencing as these feelings could escalate and impact his well-being as well as his job satisfaction.

Reggie decided to speak to the phase lead whom he works with closely day to day. He has developed a good working relationship with the phase lead, and they have worked together on planning the maths delivery for the autumn term. Due to the trusting relationship, Reggie was able to share honestly how he felt. The phase lead reassured Reggie and also explained that he needed to think about his own approach to feedback, and that Reggie needed to recognise that all feedback is intended to support him. The phase lead also suggested that Reggie work with his ECT mentor and develop a 'to do' list, which would help him organise and prioritise his work.

It was hard for Reggie to acknowledge that he needed help, but he took the steps to speak openly with a trusted colleague who he had connected well with over his first term. This enabled him to take the step of speaking to his ECT mentor in a more formal way to ensure that he was supported in prioritising and not becoming overwhelmed with the feedback being received.

Reflective task ◀◀◀

Thinking about the case study.

- Consider a time when you have felt similar to Reggie. Perhaps there has been a lot of feedback at once, or your workload has felt unmanageable. How did you draw upon your network to support you?

- Who would be your trusted colleague with whom to share concerns and worries? Remember that this is not just about someone who is friendly towards you; you are looking for someone who will give you sound advice and signpost you to good support.

- Reggie's strategy was to develop a 'to do' list but there are lots of other approaches that can help you feel in control of your work. Which strategies work for you? Are there new strategies that you could start to adopt as part of your toolkit?

See Chapter 5 for ideas about some other strategies for aspects such as prioritising, for example.

Now what?

Building networks is something that is within your control, and your networks can extend beyond your own school to the wider education community. Online opportunities to connect are a good way to develop strong networks. The activities below are suggestions to help you achieve this ambition of developing a strong network that you can draw upon throughout your career.

Practical task for tomorrow ◀◀◀

Identify one action that will influence someone in your network to help you achieve one of your short-term goals. It could be asking to collaborate with another teacher or strengthening your relationship with your TA through having a professional conversation about the day-to-day activities or how you can both work more effectively together.

Practical task for next week ◀◀◀

Talk with your ECT mentor about how you can identify expertise in others to help you achieve your goals and targets. Consider the way you are setting targets: are you also considering where expertise that you can observe or engage with is located or are your targets all about what you will do?

Practical task for the long term ◀◀◀

Engage with the wider education community such as through ECT networks on social media. Start to engage in the wider community of evidence-based practice in education. Keep considering how you can learn from others and use the expertise and experience of those immediately close to you in school and also in the wider education community.

What next? ◀◀◀

This chapter has explored how you can draw upon other people to support you in the early phase of your career as an ECT. You have had the opportunity to think about how you can deliberately create a network of people to support you in flourishing during your ECT phase and you have recognised the concept of Ubuntu, where the community in which you engage influences your own identity and sense of who you are. The intention of this chapter is to support you in realising that building positive and trusting relationships and developing a network does not just happen: you have to be proactive and seek out the most appropriate support for you. Remember that you have joined a profession where collaboration, reciprocal working and continuous feedback to improve are part of the culture. Colleagues have good intentions for you when they offer advice or feedback, and it is a helpful approach to develop an open-minded attitude towards this culture. Your school community will want to support you and so consciously connect with colleagues: appreciate them and recognise their input to your development. Also, take the time to engage with the wider education community. Following educational colleagues on Twitter, LinkedIn or similar will help you not only develop professionally but connect you to people who are experiencing similar things to you.

Further reading

Grafton, A (2022) *Great Networking: The Art and Practice of Building Authentic Professional Relationships*. London: LID Publishing.

Howard, C, Carroll, J, Owens, J and Langston, D (2020) *The School Mentor's Guide: How to Mentor New and Beginning Teachers.* London: Learning Matters, Sage Publications.

Quigley, A (2016) *The Confident Teacher: Developing Successful Habits of Mind, Body and Pedagogy.* London: Routledge.

Stone, G (2022) *Professionalism in Primary Teaching.* London: Sage.

Websites

The Elephant Times, an online magazine, is available at the following link: www.tidegloballearn ing.net/about/elephant-times (accessed 9 August 2022).

Twitter: @MrTs_NQTs

References

Bryk, A S and Schneider, B (2003) Trust in Schools: A Core Resource for School Reform. *Educational Leadership*, 60(6): 40–6.

Cialdini, R (2007) *Influence: The Psychology of Persuasion.* New York: Collins.

Donne, J (1988) *No Man is an Island.* London: Souvenir Press.

Fox, A and Wilson, E (2015) Networking and the Development of Professionals: Beginning Teachers Building Social Capital. *Teaching and Teacher Education*, 47: 93–107.

Miller, J B and Stiver, I P (1997) *The Healing Connection: How Women Form Relationships in Therapy and in Life.* Boston, MA: Beacon.

Ogude, J (2018) *Ubuntu and Personhood.* London: Africa World Press.

Rodenburg, P (2007) *Presence: How to Use Positive Energy for Success in Every Situation.* London: Penguin Group.

Shuck, S, Aususson, P, Buchanan, J, Varadharajan, M and Burke, P (2017) The Experiences of Early Career Teachers: New Initiatives and Old Problems. *Professional Development in Education*, 44(2): 209–21.

Steiha, V and Raider-Roth, M (2012) Presence in Context: Teachers' Negotiations with the Relational Environment of School. *Journal of Educational Change*, 13: 511–34.

Wilhelm, A, Woods, D, del Rosal, K and Wu, S (2020) Refining a Professional Network: Understanding First-Year Teachers' Advice Seeking. *Teacher Education Quarterly*, 47(3): 96–119.

Chapter 5   How can I look after myself?

What? (The big idea)

Work–life balance

When you start as an ECT it is important that you find time to reflect upon what aspects of your new job are going well, in addition to those items that remain an area of development. This self-appraisal of your professional status will help you celebrate your many successes but also alert you to any personal and professional demands that could affect your sense of well-being. Remember: positive well-being is vital for you to be effective as an ECT, no matter what professional task you may be engaged in. Your professional life must not be seen in isolation from that of your personal one. They are inextricably linked and, no matter how much you try, one will inevitably influence the other for good or ill. Therefore, your well-being should be seen in terms of your holistic self where all elements of your being, personal and professional (physical, emotional, mental, social, spiritual) are nurtured and protected. This will not only bring out the healthiest and most contented version of yourself but will help you to survive and thrive as an ECT.

How you organise and manage your professional practice will inevitably influence how you feel about your job and yourself. Therefore, this chapter considers how you should use your own professional systems and routines to support the efficient use of time and the tasks that you undertake in your job, and how you can collaborate with your peers when needed to provide you with the right support. It also considers how you can best protect the time you need for rest and recovery in order that you can be at your peak when providing teaching and learning for the children in your care.

Professional challenges to well-being

As an ECT, how you feel about your working practices will make a huge difference to your sense of well-being. Reports such as Schleicher (2018, p 11) have drawn links between that of *'stressful working environments'* and the effect it may have on teachers in terms of their *'motivation, self-efficacy and job commitment'*. This research makes a connection between a teacher's well-being, their physical and emotional health and those cognitive skills necessary to be effective in their professional duties (their self-efficacy).

For researchers such as Hatley and Kington (2021), ECTs like yourself may be seen to face many challenges. These include items such as the administration duties and workload associated with being a teacher. You may have already started finding tasks such as completing paperwork, eg planning, marking and assessment of pupils' progress which are fundamental to your teaching, very time-intensive. All such items can add a sense of stress to your job and will, even if it is not obvious at times, impact upon your sense of well-being. Negative well-being can manifest itself in behavioural, psychological or physical symptoms relating to work (ESP, 2018). As the Education Support Partnership (ESP) (2018) indicates, for teachers such items can lead to ill health or even individuals considering leaving the profession.

Issues around workload are not new to teachers. Support for teachers through planning, preparation and assessment (PPA) time was initiated in an attempt to reduce the recognised administrative burden on teachers. Teachers who have served in the profession for many years will have had time to adapt to the demands of educational change and many will have developed effective strategies to deal with such issues. As an ECT you too will develop strategies and practices that work best for you. One example of such a strategy is timeboxing. This is a task-orientated strategy which helps you focus on completing priority-identified items. Timeboxing encourages you to estimate how long each item will take. It enables you to create a prioritised list which then requires you stick to this time when completing it. For items that remain incomplete you then review the progress you have made and, if necessary, reallocate more time for this task's completion. Another strategy for reviewing the importance of tasks is the use of the Eisenhower Matrix (University of Hull, 2022). Such a matrix, as shown in Table 5.1, confronts the user with a consideration of the importance of tasks and their completion using the words 'important' and 'urgent'. Urgent tasks are items that need completing immediately or in the shortest timeframe possible, while important tasks can be completed as soon as urgent tasks have been dealt with. Positioning your tasks in each quadrant of this matrix may help you prioritise things in your 'to do' list.

Table 5.1 Eisenhower Matrix

	Urgent	**Not urgent**
Important	Do it now!	Choose when to do it later. Assign time in your 'to do' list or diary.
Not important	Only do it when the above work is done. If it is not related to the setting, can you ask someone else to do it?	Disregard it for now. Do not do it if you are completely committed to something else.

Reflective task ◀◀◀

How effective are you at using personalised systems and routines to support your efficient use of time and task management?

First, jot down the tasks that you currently encounter on a daily basis. For example, these items may include planning, marking and preparing resources for lessons. Now using the prompts below reflect upon the tasks you have recorded.

- What are your current strategies to help you deal with these tasks, given the demands placed on your time?

- Which strategies work best and are there others that need revision to make them more effective and efficient?

- If you were to alter the allocation of time given to these tasks or the time when you do them, would it free up time to help you be more effective in your job?

- If tasks seem too big, break them down into manageable chunks.

- Prioritise tasks and arrange your workload in order of the most important. Remember, not all tasks fit neatly into a must-do box.

- Give tasks dedicated time and avoid procrastination. Try and identify if there are any tasks that keep getting avoided or simply not done. Consider: why do they prove so problematic? Do you need to allocate more time to them or do you really need to do them? Can you delegate this task?

- Consider: can a task be put on hold if it does not have any impact upon you or others?

- Record your 'to do' list in a diary, web-based calendar or a phone or computer app.

Classroom management and well-being

As well as issues around manageable workload for teachers, authors such as Hatley and Kington (2021) identify challenges linked to supporting pupils with additional needs and behaviour management issues. For many experienced teachers, this facet of teaching may continue to prove a challenge even if they have been in teaching for many years. If you have built up trust, are planning for your pupils' needs/attainment and have a good rapport with your pupils, you are likely to be managing behaviour successfully. However, if things seem to be going less well, it is important that you seek help as soon as possible from your mentor, phase leader, SENDCo or headteacher. You have a right to receive such help and support and if you do not seek this out, such challenges may reduce your self-confidence and well-being. Support may be found through provision such as coaching and mentoring by your peers and/or, if needed, focused professional development. This assistance may also take the form of professional counselling, which may be delivered in your setting or via an outside provider.

Sharing the load

As you start your new job try not to be daunted by the workload. Any such worries could affect your well-being. As an ECT you will be walking in the footsteps of other teachers who have gone before you. With this in mind, you will be able to tap into a wealth of curriculum-specific resources which can help relieve the burden around planning, its associated workload and its impact upon your well-being. Such support may be found in terms of online forums and blogs. Many of these are written by professionals for professionals and they offer a wealth of practical support and a means to share expert resources to support your teaching. For example, Kaytie Holdstock (2022) has designed an online space to share art ideas to support primary school teachers with creative ideas for the classroom.

Many of your teaching colleagues will be eager to share their planning and resources linked to the curriculum and topics they teach. You will be joining a nurturing profession where individuals are eager to support their new colleagues in any way they can. You will be encouraged to collaborate with peers in shared planning. If you are in a larger school, parallel year or subject teachers will meet with you to share the workload and expectations of planning.

Your school will also have many shared resources such as published and school schemes of work and pupil textbooks and workbooks. Many of these items may in turn be supported by planned activities and worksheets to consolidate and deepen pupils' learning. In addition to this, web-based platforms may also be a useful resource or school-adopted means to access schemes of work and resources.

Personal well-being

From a personal perspective you will find the demands on your home life and health will inevitably ebb and flow as you progress during your first years of teaching. Practical issues such as finding accommodation, the length of a daily commute and a wish to find quality time with friends and family may all have to be juggled with your school commitments. For some of you, ongoing underlying health issues may also add to a feeling that teaching and managing a personal life is a real balancing act.

Personal well-being starts with knowing how to work smarter, not harder. It is about what you can do to make your work time-efficient and often when to say no. Consider: are there more effective strategies or routines you could employ to help with what will always feel limited time? You will also have to, if you have not already done so, learn to master the art of delegation in order to help you cope with certain aspects of your workload. Remember, as time goes on things will get easier. You will have done certain things more than once, for example, the organisation behind parents' evening. All these experiences will help you to manage your workload and will help you maintain a healthy work–life balance. You will, as you gain more experience, be able to strengthen the boundaries you set between school and work. This will provide the key to developing greater resilience against stress. It is important that you find times when you are free from thinking about your job. Try and set yourself a clear schedule of the time when you will not be working. Do not be tempted to dip into work during those times, though this is easier said than done. Remember that you will do your job better if your batteries are fully charged, both physically and mentally. If you are physically active, it can provide a means of ameliorating the stresses and strains of everyday life. Prioritise activities you enjoy such as walking, dancing, yoga or going to the gym. Whatever your chosen activities, either indoors or outdoors, they are likely to have clear positive psychological benefits.

Reflective task ◀◀◀

How have you started to support and protect your own well-being both professionally and personally in terms of strategies and routines? Using the table below consider the following.

- What issues or feelings do you currently have in relation to teaching that may be impacting on your sense of positive well-being?

- How are these feelings manifesting themselves?

- What can you do to mitigate against these?

Below is a sample (Table 5.2) which can be used for this audit. It includes an example to get you started.

Table 5.2 Personal audit

Symptom affecting your well-being	Telltale signs	Self-care strategies
Example *Feeling anxious before you return to work after a holiday.*	*Feeling nervous, restless, tense or negative thoughts towards a task or situation. Having trouble concentrating and feeling lethargic.*	*Front load the beginning of your holiday with tasks that need to be done before you return to work. This will free you of the worry and dread of having to engage with these items just before you return.*

So what? ◀ ◀ ◀

Why is it interesting?

Working with children can have many positive benefits and rewards for your sense of well-being. These can include watching young learners have those lightbulb moments and making a real difference to the children in your care. However, as studies such as the ESP (2018) have shown, teaching can also have a negative impact upon your well-being. This can be linked to factors such as dealing with paperwork, dealing with poor learning behaviours and the ongoing changes linked to government policies driving change in education (ESP, 2018). Even if it does not feel obvious, such factors can unknowingly affect your sense of positive well-being. It can result in feelings of being unable to cope, feeling the strain and not being able to do your job to the best of your ability. It is important to remember, however, that you are part of a team and the school will be there to help you and support you if there is a need (Howard et al, 2020).

As an ECT you must do all you can to find the means and strategies to enhance your own personal and professional resilience in order to protect your well-being. On a personal level, this can be achieved by being alert to your own emotional self-awareness (as outlined by Goleman, 1996). This can help you acknowledge how you are feeling and how such emotions are affecting your daily life and relationships with others. For some people, a sense of positive well-being can be achieved by engaging with the practice of mindfulness (a useful starting point for considering this can be found at www.mindful.org). It can provide them with a means of emotional self-regulation, self-efficacy and well-being. As research demonstrates (Meiklejohn et al, 2012), for teachers it can help not only support an ability to manage classroom behaviours, but can enhance relationships with other individuals.

An awareness of your emotional state can also help you make positive decisions that can support you when doing your job. Such emotion-focused coping (Lazurus and Folkman, 1984; Aulén et al, 2021) may take the form of either cognitive or behavioural coping. In terms of cognitive coping this may lead to a re-evaluation of your areas of focus or for behavioural coping, building in time to relax such as with family and friends.

For researchers such as Lazurus and Folkman (1984) and Aulén et al (2021), coping for individuals can also take the form of problem-focused coping strategies. Techniques such as solution-focused thinking can help develop such ideas.

With solution-focused thinking individuals try:

» positively focusing on the issue in question;

» seeing problems as an opportunity;

» considering what solutions may have worked so far (with some consideration of the scale of such impact);

» possible solutions that have been identified in order to find out a workable solution to the problem;

» thinking creatively and differently.

Remember that sometimes there may be no easy or quick fixes to the issues you face. At these times it is important you know who you can turn to. This could include your mentor, peers, headteacher and even outside agencies such as your union or a counselling service to gain their advice and support to make things more manageable and tolerable. Remember, experienced colleagues will have a depth of experience in such issues and will be able to signpost you to the best help and support available.

Reflective task ◀◀◀

To identify roles or tasks which may impact your well-being, try creating a timeline of the things that must be done on a weekly, termly and yearly basis. Consider how you feel about these duties and how effectively you are currently dealing with them. Start by using the following reflective prompts.

• Think about the tasks you do in a typical week, term and year.

• Which of those tasks must be done now, could be done later on or can be put off until needed?

• Consider: which tasks do you enjoy and look forward to and which tasks would you like to put off?

• Use a ranking scale of 1 (most enjoy) to 10 (least enjoy) to place them on a continuum.

• What routines and systems do you currently use to help you deal with these tasks?

- Are these routines and systems making these tasks feel manageable, helping you use time effectively, and do they help you to feel more positively about these items?

- Are there any alternative solutions you could try to deliver an improvement on how you feel currently about these tasks?

- Now put what you have learned about yourself and how you manage your professional duties in the structured Table 5.3 provided below to form a reflective action planner for the year.

Table 5.3 Reflective action planner

Timeframe	Ranking scale regarding enjoyment	Current means to deal with the task or routine	Alternatives I might try
Weekly tasks			
Termly tasks			
Yearly tasks			

Case study ◀◀◀

Barbara's story

This case study is from an ECT who is one term into their teaching career.

Barbara was happy in her job. However, the one thing that she found time consuming and would ideally love to have put off was the marking of her pupils' work. She often spent quite a lot of time in the evening adding reflective comments as well as correcting misconceptions, grammatical and spelling errors. This commitment of time often meant that Barbara had to delay doing other jobs on her 'to do' list. What frustrated Barbara most is that though she gave detailed feedback, often pupils did not spend time engaging with her marking comments or, she felt, even gave them a cursory glance. She believed that her marking gave valuable formative feedback but the time spent on it as well as its seeming lack of impact was really affecting her mood and how she viewed her role.

If Barbara continued with this current practice, she may have found that her feelings could have started to affect her motivation towards her job and even her health. She needed to reconsider her personal systems and routines used for this task so that she could find a more efficient use of her time. She could also talk to her peers to see if they have used a marking system which could be beneficial to her.

As a result of this review, Barbara implemented several new systems which seemed to be successful not only in terms of making her feel more positive towards this task but also releasing time for her to either relax more or catch up on other tasks that were not deemed such a priority. These systems included once a week asking pupils to peer assess themselves after they had completed their work by placing their books in one of three piles (totally understood, found understanding alright and did not understand). Barbara then targeted the 'did not understand' books with deep marking (and light touch marked the others). Barbara also asked pupils to read her marking and then write a comment to confirm what they learned from it.

Reflective task ◀◀◀

Consider the reflective prompts below with regard to your own practice and use them to reflect upon your own time management and its value to your teaching and learning.

- What tasks or practices are you currently finding time consuming?

- How does the time invested enhance the quality of your teaching and learning?

- Are there times in your school day that could be freed up for better use? If so, when and how?

Now what? ◀ ◀ ◀

Looking forward

The practical tasks suggested below are a starting point for an ongoing reflection of your systems, routines and practices. If these are proving effective, they can unlock valuable time and effort that can be used to enhance your professional and personal life.

Practical task for tomorrow ◀◀◀

Make time to talk to your mentor or peers about your daily practices and routines, including those that are going well and any that you are finding particularly problematic. Ask them for suggestions from their own practices that might be useful to release valuable professional and personal time for you. Consider whether any of their suggestions could be helpful to you and, if so, implement them.

Practical task for next week ◀◀◀

Review how your routines and practices are affecting how you feel about your week. Determine which tasks are most important and which ones are less important or could be targeted for later in the week. Use the blank template of the Eisenhower Matrix (as outlined earlier) or create your own to help you prioritise your workload for the week.

	Urgent	Not urgent
Important		
Not important		

Practical task for the long term ◀◀◀

Start to plan ahead for those one-off tasks that will come up in the year, such as parents' evenings and writing reports. Often these times will, when they happen, have an impact upon your personal relaxation times such as holiday or an evening. It is better to plan ahead for potential challenges they may create rather than trying to deal with them when they happen. See what tips and advice your colleagues can offer in how they best deal with these types of events. For example, before some teachers start report writing they often ask pupils to reflect upon how they feel their year has gone. They then ask children to record these thoughts on a child-friendly version of a report format they have created. This form can include, for example, subjects the children have enjoyed and personal achievements in the year. This information can then be used to enrich pupil reports by providing these teachers with the additional child's perspective on their progress.

What next?

This chapter has conveyed a key message which centres around the importance of protecting your well-being so as to promote effectiveness and self-efficacy in your teaching role. It is important to remember that your professional life should not be seen in isolation from your personal one. One will inevitably impact upon the other, so it is important you prioritise the protection of each so that you can enjoy and thrive in both. By developing your own professional systems and routines, you will be able to support your own efficient use of time and task management. These strategies, alongside collaboration and support from your peers, will help secure your effective and efficient professional practice, which can only be to the benefit of you and the children in your care. Remember that as a teacher you will be on a continuous learning journey and this will involve reappraising your practice to find out what works best for you. Nothing will remain static, and this is important if you are to grow professionally and protect your well-being.

Further reading

Allies, S (2021) *Supporting Teacher Well-being: A Practical Guide for Primary Teachers and School Leaders*. Abingdon: Routledge.

Bethune, A and Kell, E A (2020) *Little Guide for Teachers: Teacher Well-being and Self-care*. London: SAGE Publications.

Greer, J (2020) *Essential Guides for Early Career Teachers: Workload – Taking Ownership of Your Teaching*. St Albans: Critical Publishing.

Jennings, P (2015) *Mindfulness for Teachers*. New York: W W Norton & Company.

Perryman, J and Calvert, G (2020) What Motivates People to Teach, and Why Do They Leave? Accountability, Performativity and Teacher Retention. *British Journal of Educational Studies*, 68(1): 3–23.

Price, S (2019) *Essential Guides for Early Career Teachers: Mental Well-being and Self-care*. St Albans: Critical Publishing.

Weare, K (2015) *What Works in Promoting Social and Emotional Well-being and Responding to Mental Health Problems in School?* London: National Children's Bureau.

Welsh Assembly Government (2018) Staff Health & Well-being. [online] Available at: https://gov.wales/sites/default/files/publications/2018-03/staff-health-and-wellbeing.pdf (accessed 28 May 2022).

References

Aulén, A-M, Pakarinen, E, Taru, F and Lerkkanen, M-J (2021) Teacher Coping Profiles in Relation to Teacher Well-being: A Mixed Method Approach. *Teaching and Teacher Education*, 102: 1–10.

Education Support Partnership (ESP) (2018) Teacher Well-being Index 2018. [online] Available at: www.educationsupport.org.uk/media/drdlozbf/teacher_wellbeing_index_2018.pdf (accessed 15 August 2022).

Goleman, D (1996) *Emotional Intelligence: Why It Can Matter More Than IQ*. London: Bloomsbury.

Hatley, J and Kington, A (2021) The Influence of Support for Early Career Teachers on Their Decision to Remain in the Teaching Profession. [online] Available at: https://my.chartered.coll ege/impact_article/the-influence-of-support-for-early-career-teachers-on-their-decision-to-remain-in-the-teaching-profession (accessed 9 August 2022).

Holdstock, K (2022) Sharing Visual Arts Inspiration. [online] Available at: www.accessart.org. uk/kaytie-holdstock (accessed 2 June 2022).

Howard, C, Burton, M and Levermore, D (2020) *Children's Mental Health and Emotional Well-being in Primary Schools: A Whole School Approach.* 2nd ed. Primary Teaching Now. London: Learning Matters, Sage Publications.

Lazurus, R S and Folkman, S (1984) *Stress, Appraisal and Coping.* New York: Springer.

Meiklejohn, J, Philips, C, Freedman, M, Griffin, M, Biegel, G, Roach, A, Frank, J, Burke, C, Pinger, L, Soloway, G, Isberg, R, Sibinga, E, Grossman, L and Saltzman, A (2012) Integrating Mindfulness Training into K–12 Education: Fostering the Resilience of Teachers and Students. *Mindfulness*, 3: 291–307.

Schleicher, A (2018) *Valuing Our Teachers and Raising Their Status: How Communities Can Help*. Paris: OECD Publishing.

University of Hull (2022) Introduction to University Study: Priority Matrices. [online] Available at: https://libguides.hull.ac.uk/introduction/matrix (accessed 22 May 2022).

Chapter 6   Advice from ECT mentors for your ECT years: this is just the beginning

What? (The big idea)

Throughout this book you have considered many aspects of being an ECT. You have considered how you are developing your own professional identity as a teacher, how you develop a professional network and your place within an education learning community. You have had the opportunity to think about how you can work with the people around you and use the structure of the ECT programme to help you develop as a wonderful teacher in your own context.

In this chapter key themes are drawn together and the voices of established teachers, ECT mentors and senior leaders from across the school phases and from different geographical areas are shared, providing advice for you in your ECT phase and into your teaching career. You will have opportunity to reflect on those key themes that professionals in school are offering as advice to you.

This is just the beginning is a helpful way to think about your ECT phase. You will have high expectations for yourself and high expectations for the opportunities you will be given in your new role. Remember that you are at the beginning of the journey. Sometimes you may get things wrong and sometimes things may seem overwhelming. Develop strategies for positive self-talk, learning from mistakes and drawing upon the advice and guidance of more experienced colleagues. You also need to develop good habits for your own well-being. There are several places you can go to explore how to develop those healthy habits. Sally Price (2019) has written a book in this ECT series which supports you in reflecting upon your well-being habits and provides evidence-based approaches for you to embed in your own routines and approaches. Similarly, Suzanne Allies (2021) provides advice to support you in assessing your well-being and provides practical resources for you to develop positive actions. Suzanne has made several of these resources available on her website (see 'Further reading' on p 79), and the 'steps to success' resource is a particularly useful format that you could use as part of your ECT development.

So what? ◀ ◀ ◀

Surviving and thriving

At the beginning of this book in Chapter 1 the notion of surviving and thriving in your ECT years (Jacklin et al, 2006) was introduced. This chapter explores authentic advice from ECT mentors which will support you in establishing effective habits and attitudes to form a foundation for surviving those first new experiences. The advice also offers some inspiration to help you thrive and flourish in a career that is worthwhile and fulfilling. As you read the advice, consider some of those earlier reflections you have undertaken in this book:

>> what has motivated you to become a teacher?

>> what hopes and aspirations do you have for the children and young people in your class?

>> how will you develop your own knowledge and skills so that you are effective and fulfilled in your work?

Case study 4 on page 76 provides a good starting point as we consider how it feels to be right at the beginning of your career. In the case study, Adaeze talks about being 'consciously incompetent'. This phrase is from a model developed by Gordon Training International (Adams, 2021) and is an interesting way to consider how you develop new skills (see Figure 6.1).

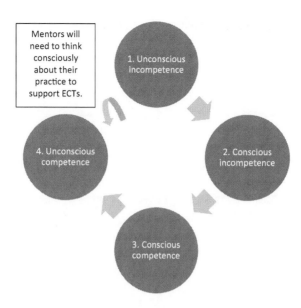

Figure 6.1 Competency model (summarised from Adams, 2021)

The concept is that there are four stages to learning a skill.

1. To begin with you are unconsciously incompetent – that is, you are not good
    at the skill, but you don't realise you are not good at the skill. In fact, you may
    not realise that you need that skill. You may have heard the phrase 'ignorance
    is bliss' and this stage is like that. You may have experienced this when you
    first went into a classroom and realised that you needed skills in behaviour
    management or relationship development, for example, but until that moment
    you had perhaps not recognised these skills as essential aspects in the role
    of teacher.

2. The next is the stage that Adaeze refers to: conscious incompetence. This is
    where you realise that you are not as good as you want to be. This can be an
    uncomfortable place when you can intellectually understand what you need
    to do but your practice in that aspect is not yet competent. However, this is a
    place where learning and developing can happen quickly because there is a
    motivation to get better and seek the feedback that Asif talks about in case
    study 1 (below).

3. As your skill develops you will become consciously competent. At this stage, you are able to work independently but you have to focus and concentrate on getting this right. The ECT stage is a time of moving to this step where you are increasingly confident and competent in the classroom and you are developing your independence as a teacher. However, this stage of conscious competence can be tiring with the focus of energy and concentration needed. Your ECT mentor and school colleagues will be mindful of this and will recall their own experiences during this part of their career. Share with them if this is how you are feeling and they will be able to reassure and support you.

4. Finally, and this is likely to be a characteristic you observe in your ECT mentor, there is unconscious competence. The skill is so well practised and embedded that you no longer have to think about it. It is just part of what you do, and you start to feel confident and comfortable (Paige et al, 2020) in your classroom practice. In the model below, this final stage is looped back to show that mentors need to consciously think about their practice to support you as an ECT by breaking down what success looks like and you will have opportunity to do this as you deconstruct practice in your mentor conversations.

The rest of this chapter is focused on the case study advice from ECT mentors. In case study 2 Evan talks about his beliefs that education has a *transformative power* and that *excellent teaching* makes a difference. He also highlights how important it is to celebrate the *small wins*. These aspects are motivational for Evan, and help him strive forward in his pursuit for excellent teaching and when there are more challenging times. It is intended that these case studies will help you think about your motivations and provide you with some supportive guidance.

Case study 1 ◀◀◀

Introducing Asif, an ECT mentor

Asif is an assistant headteacher in Worcestershire and is also the ECT mentor in his school. Asif works in a small Church of England primary school which is part of a larger academy trust. Asif had a career previously working for a solicitors' office but made a decision to follow his ambition of teaching by re-training five years ago. He has moved quickly into leadership roles and reflects on the key skills and attitudes that have supported him to be successful.

Advice from Asif: be prepared and view feedback as your friend

Having been an NQT/ECT only four years ago, I know exactly how you might feel in the weeks leading up to the first day of term: the excitement of starting your first job with a class of your own, eagerness to get going and for me ... full of nerves. However, you will be pleased to know, these nerves soon disappeared once I stepped foot in the classroom.

My advice for any new ECT would be as follows.

- Be as prepared as you can be before the first day of term. Speak with your school and other class teachers and try and get as much information as you can about how they deliver the curriculum. This will enable you to hit the ground running rather than chasing your tail with planning.

- Use your ECT and PPA time wisely. A lot of ECTs use this time only for planning, which I think is a huge mistake. Ask to go and see as many other teachers as you can delivering and modelling their delivery of different areas of the curriculum. This will enable you to see good practice as well as enabling you to reflect on your own.

- Feedback is your friend – be open to observations and feedback. I appreciate the emotions of being observed; I still fill up with anxiety when someone comes to watch me teach. However, as an ECT and a teacher, you must get used to it pretty quickly, as it will be a regular occurrence. For me, feedback can only be seen as a positive thing. There will be things you are doing well, there will also be things you need to work on and, as hard as it is, try not to take these things too negatively. Feedback enables you to reflect on your practice and make excellent progress within the profession. Therefore, ask as many people as you can (including heads, assistant heads, SLT and subject leaders) to come and watch you and actively seek feedback. It is in your best interest and the school's!

- Finally, if in doubt, ask. There is no such thing as a silly question. If you are not sure about something ... ask. It is better to ask for advice from someone within the school than simply do what you think is right.

Reflective task ◀◀◀

After reading case study 1, think about your circumstances and how Asif's ideas can be useful to you.

- How organised and well prepared are you? Are you someone who is always rushing at the last minute or do you have good systems for being prepared?

- Reflect upon the way you manage and organise your time and whether any adjustments would help you to prioritise and become more organised.

- How do you respond to feedback? Do you find it easy, or do you sometimes feel a little defensive or even deflated after spending a lot of time on preparation and planning?

- Take time to look at your school's curriculum intent statements and how the curriculum has been sequenced in a particular subject. Can you identify how the sequencing of the curriculum supports learning?

- Talk with your ECT mentor about your understanding of the curriculum intent in a particular subject and your plans for implementing the curriculum. Talk through how you will know that children are learning and making progress throughout the sequence of lessons.

Top tips ◀◀◀

- One of Stephen Covey's effective habits is to prioritise important over urgent, or to think 'first thing first' (Covey, 2004). We are often so busy it is hard to know where to start with our 'to do' list, but by developing habits of evaluating what is important then we are more likely to be successful and have a greater impact. If you look back to Chapter 5 in this book, there are some practical ideas for time management and prioritising, such as timeboxing or the use of a priority matrix. Try these approaches and see if they help you in managing your time well.

- Before engaging with a feedback conversation, make sure your own mindset is one of growth (Dweck, 2017). In adopting a growth mindset (as described by Carol Dweck) you will develop resilience and perseverance when things don't go as well as anticipated and you will embrace challenges, rather than avoid them.

Deliberate practice

As you read through the case studies, some common themes emerge. In case study 1, Asif talks about how you need to view feedback as your friend. This theme highlights how important feedback is to your professional development and the importance of developing a positive attitude to feedback. You are joining a profession where feedback and action planning are part of the culture and the approach to improvement. However, feedback is not an activity in isolation. There is growing research in the area of deliberate practice (Deans for Impact, 2022) as an approach to developing expertise. It is an approach that challenges the concept of experience being the key driver to expertise and improvement. There are some key steps to developing expertise in the deliberate practice model, as shown in Figure 6.2.

1. Push beyond your comfort zone

2. Set specific goals

3. Focus on practice activities

4. Receive and respond to feedback

5. Develop mental models of expertise

Figure 6.2 A summary of deliberate practice (adapted from Deans for Impact, 2022)

You will see from the five areas of deliberate practice that self-evaluation and reflection, alongside specific target setting, works with the focused feedback you will gain from others. Therefore, in deliberate practice, your responsibility and active participation in becoming effective as a teacher is very important. You are not relying on someone else's judgement solely and being a passive participant in the process of knowing where your strengths and areas for development lie. Instead, you have a realistic view of how you are performing, and you push yourself beyond that comfort zone, take time to rehearse (focus on practice activities) and you are open and responsive to the feedback you receive.

In the next case study, Evan offers some ideas around celebrating the small wins which can support you in your motivation and in developing a growth mindset.

Case study 2 ◄◄◄

Introducing Evan, an ITT and ECT mentor

Evan works in Bexley, London. He is currently the English lead and has been a mentor for trainee teachers and ECTs in the different schools in which he has worked. He has worked with many ECTs and enjoys the interpersonal aspects of this role.

Advice from Evan: 'Screw your courage to the sticking place'

Ten years seems like a long time since I started my ECT years; however I can still remember the feelings of those first steps into teaching. The nerves of starting a new school; excitement in thinking about what I would be teaching; the bold ambitions of what kind of teacher I would be. These might be feelings that are resonating with you now as you take your own first steps. So, what advice can I give you to help smooth the transition from trainee to ECT?

- *Take the small wins. We all like to think that we can be perfect straight away. Tick the boxes, put in the work and be perfect ... now! Teaching is very rarely like this – especially at the start. There can be times where it feels like you are running towards a perpetually moving finish line, constantly just out of reach. It's at these times where you need to stop, reflect on the small wins and think about the impact small steps are having on your larger journey.*

- *'Children do not learn from people they do not like' (Pierson, 2013). If you haven't yet watched Rita Pierson's TED talk: Every Child Needs a Champion, then do so right after finishing this chapter. It may seem obvious, but it is true – children very rarely learn from teachers they do not like. Does this mean I am advocating you pulling out your old box of circus tricks to entertain your classes? No. But think about the relationship you build with those in your care and the long-term impact a positive academic relationship can have.*

- *Be prepared for anything. It may seem obvious but the more prepared you are the easier time you will have. In my career, I find myself asking more and more 'But what about plan C?'. Within a busy classroom too often plan A and B go out of the window within a matter of moments. Be pragmatic in thinking about the 'what ifs ...' and plan accordingly. You may never need to use them (if you are that lucky) but knowing where to pivot if needed will save you any moments of panic where things may not be going how you would like.*

- *'Screw your courage to the sticking place' (Shakespeare's Macbeth Act 1, Scene 7 in Watts, 1992). Finally, remember that you have chosen to come into this profession for a reason. Probably because you realise the transformative power that education can have. Stand strong in your passion for this vocation, have courage in your belief that excellent teaching makes a difference and enjoy being in the classroom!*

Reflective task ◀◀◀

- Are you recognising the 'small wins'? In deliberate practice, goals should be specific so that they are tangible and achievable. Are you breaking down what you need to achieve into those manageable chunks?

- Think about how you are building relationships with the children in your class. How are you demonstrating to all children that you have an interest in them in a holistic way? How are you showing that you care in your interactions?

- If your goals seem too big or unachievable, use some of your ECT mentoring time to talk about how you can improve in this area. Your mentor will want to support you in effective goal/target setting so that you are able to build upon your achievements and identify effective ways to improve. Getting this right will make a big difference to your success!

- In Chapter 1 you thought about the interlink between professional and personal (Day et al, 2006; Meijer at al, 2009) for you as the teacher in building relationships. In building relationships think about how you can share something of yourself with the children, such as a hobby you enjoy. Maintaining professional boundaries is really important; however, to create connections with the children in your class you will want to share something of yourself with them.

Case study 3 ◀◀◀

Introducing Louisa: executive headteacher in Special School settings

Louisa has been in education for many years, starting off her career in mainstream and then working as a teacher, headteacher and now executive headteacher in Special School education. Louisa has a strong commitment to supporting trainee teachers and ECTs through mentoring as well as supporting teacher training programmes with specialist sessions.

Advice from Louisa: developing your identity and belonging

It is about 20 years since I was in my newly qualified teacher year, but I remember it very vividly.

I was really excited to have my own class and was pleased to be starting my teaching career at the same time as two other NQTs. We were very passionate about teaching and dedicated to lifelong learning. If there was a course to have or training to receive, we loved to do that.

One of my strong memories was realising that the level of observation and supervision that you experience through training is not there once you have your own class, so developing good working habits is essential to ensure you maintain a great standard in what you do. Planning your teaching week to make life manageable for the children and yourself was also a real focus. I tried to have a positive mixture of practical and written learning throughout each week, so it was engaging for the learners, but also workable as the teacher – this helped me to keep on top of my marking and feedback workload.

It was also really important to me that I was allowed to develop a sense of identity and belonging to the school; again, this is something that brought me great enjoyment. I wanted to lead clubs, take part in competitions, work with other teachers and learn new things. I found that throwing myself into school life created happiness – I really felt the more I put in, the more I got from it. This wasn't about developing a work–life balance or a focus on well-being that we think about today, but for me I was able to gain well-being and happiness from fully engaging – I really enjoyed it. If this helps you, volunteer to do things! Ask your headteacher if you can start a club – but start one thing at a time and enjoy it.

Before I started my teaching year and still today the things that really helped me were being prepared, and prioritising that. It was great that I was able to get into my classroom before the year began, as I was able to organise the room, find useful resources and label everything. This all really helped – it meant that everyone in the room could find everything, it helped the children to be independent and gave them a sense of order and responsibility for their surroundings.

As I mentioned, I was one of three NQTs starting at the same time and we were spread throughout the school – but forging good working (and what have developed to be lifelong) friendships was also a really positive thing to do. I see teaching as a relational profession, and developing the skill of having professional relationships with others (at every level) is something worth thinking about. My advice is to find your like-minded colleagues, so you feel you can safely discuss and debrief, meet and talk with colleagues who share different viewpoints – knowing we can learn from each other – and be a good communicator – present your best self while you are at work – asking when you don't understand things, and taking a chance to try new things.

I think for me, it's key to remember if you are enjoying yourself, the children will enjoy themselves and everyone will learn far more.

Reflective task ◀◀◀

In case study 3 Louisa emphasises the importance of finding your place in the school community and gaining a sense of fun and fulfilment in being part of the wider life of your school. Reflect on how you have engaged with the wider school community so far.

- What are the things you enjoy doing? Could you bring this to an aspect of your school community? Perhaps it is music, dance, art or sport that you could offer as part of an extra-curriculum club. Or maybe you would like to get more involved in charity fundraising at your school or supporting productions or events.

Top tip ◀◀◀

It can be very fulfilling and enjoyable to get involved in things beyond the classroom. The children also have an opportunity to see you in a different way when not part of the formality of lessons. Do choose what you get involved in so that these aspects which should bring variety and fun to your work life do not put additional pressure on you.

It is not the end ... it is just the beginning

This chapter and this book are coming towards the end. However, for you this is just the beginning of a very exciting career. The intention in this book has been to provide you with some key things to think about during your ECT years and to also provide you with some helpful models and ideas which you can talk about further with your ECT mentor and other experienced colleagues who are supporting you. Some of the themes emerging from the advice from established teachers and ECT mentors in this chapter have included the following.

- Be prepared and develop effective organisational and prioritisation habits.

- Learn from others, eg watching other professionals or engaging with inspiring podcasts/blogs/Twitter.

- Develop your relational networks with colleagues and consider how you develop the relationships with the children in your class.

- Feedback is positive and having a growth mindset around feedback will help you in becoming an effective practitioner.

- Take opportunities for CPD.

- Develop good habits for your own well-being.

- Remember why you became a teacher and continue to be motivated by the wonderful opportunities to make a difference.

There will be specific aspects in this chapter that will have resonated most closely with you. To conclude this chapter, which has focused on the voices of ECT mentors, here are ten top tips from Adaeze (case study 4).

Case study 4 ◀◀◀

Introducing Adaeze: senior mental health lead and mentor

Adaeze is the senior mental health lead at her school in Woolwich, London. She teaches English and is the Head of Year. Adaeze has worked with ECTs and trainee teachers in a mentoring capacity and has a deep commitment to their development.

Advice from Adaeze: *If I knew then what I know now …*

Although it has been a decade since removing my NQT pants (as I like to call them), I remember the feeling well. The feeling of being new to anything is often a daunting one, but just remember that the feeling of nervousness is physiologically almost the same as the feeling of excitement, so keep that in mind and try to channel that excitement. If I knew then what I know now, my top ten tips would be these.

1. *Be kind to yourself. You will make mistakes. You will feel consciously incompetent. Try and be as kind and patient to yourself as you are with your students.*

2. *Find your best time for work and ensure that your time is spent on high-impact tasks. For example, do not spend 15 minutes marking a piece of work that the students will spend 15 seconds reading. I never mark at night because I inevitably spend longer on this task as my body and brain are both tired. I always mark first thing as I am faster, and I have no choice but to stick to the deadline.*

3. *Find your routines early on. Students need reliability and respond to consistency. Don't give them a 'Rules lesson' on your first day but talk to them about expectations: the rules will be established in your regular routines and procedures.*

4. *Choose your battles.*

5. *Have friends outside of teaching – teachers like to talk shop and it can become consuming. Socialising with your colleagues is important but so is having a life outside of school. With this in mind, try to do all of your work in school – and I never work in my bedroom.*

6. *I am Adaeze first and teacher second. Staff and students need to see this. If you see Mohammed in the cheese aisle in Sainsbury's, say hi! However, don't give too much of yourself as remember the children are reliant on the routines and procedures and never rely too heavily on personality.*

7. Try to find the positive and avoid the negative. Positivity attracts positivity and students thrive in a positive environment. As the students enter a room, verbally acknowledge what you are happy to see. At the end of a lesson, have you awarded the same number of positive points compared to negative? Are you spending time with colleagues that share this approach? The truth is, you can't have a life of positivity while spending a lot of time with people who drag you down.

8. Find a mentor, a champion. As Rita Pierson states, 'every child needs a champion!' and so do you! Listen to their feedback and don't take this as criticism. There is always room for improvement, even in most outstanding lessons.

9. Never hold grudges or take things too personally. You will encounter students whose behaviour could be considered rude and I assure you that, at times, this will feel like a personal attack. Remember, students will always respond better to routines and procedures over emotions. Also, consider whether Johnny has conflict management modelled for them at home. Shouting at Johnny and demanding respect may trigger a negative response due to their home environment. Follow the school procedure policy and always follow up with the student. In my opinion, the best approach is a restorative one: find out why the student has behaved in that way and explain in a rational manner how this made you feel. Tell them that you did not think this was kind and see what their response is. There are lots of great resources online on restorative approaches in education and talk to whoever oversees CPD if this is something you are interested in.

10. My final tip is remembering why you chose to be a teacher. Surely you have a love for learning and, in this job, the learning never stops. Invest time, including your own, in CPD and never become complacent.

Now what?

Practical task for tomorrow ◀◀◀

- In case studies 2 and 4 both Evan and Adaeze recommended Rita Pierson, an educator based in the US, who has been an inspiration to them. Take some time to listen to either Pierson (2013) or an educator who inspires you.

- Make some notes of the key aspects that inspire you. There may be some key phrases that resonate with you and that may help you throughout your career.

Practical task for next week ◀◀◀

All of the mentors in the case studies talked about being organised. In case study 1, Asif recommends that you plan out your PPA time and think carefully about how you use that time. Asif suggests that you might want to observe others in that time or engage further with the curriculum so that you have a strong understanding of the curriculum intent and implementation.

- With your ECT mentor, create a timetable of how you will use your PPA and ECT time over the next term. Sometimes you will want time for planning and assessing, but also map in activities that will support your wider understanding of these areas. Your timetable might look like the table below, for example.

Table 6.1 A template for planning your ECT time

Date	Activity	Time needed	What I want to achieve
	Observe phase lead teaching science	40 minutes	To develop my understanding of how to manage practical science tasks.
	Look at tracking data with assessment lead	30 minutes	To understand how assessment data is recorded and used in the school.

Practical task for the long term ◀◀◀

Changing our habits take time. In fact, psychologists (Lally et al, 2010) suggest it can take up to two months to establish new behaviours and habits. Therefore, think carefully about some of the well-being advice given in this chapter.

- Use the resources provided by Suzanne Allies on her website (www.support ingteacherwellbeing.wordpress.com) and think about which of your habits or behaviours need adjusting or developing.

- Start to deliberately incorporate those habits and behaviours into your routines. It might be making time for exercise, or pursuing a hobby, or taking 'time out' from work and doing something relaxing. Work out what is right for you and start to include it in your routines.

What next?

This chapter has shared some practical tips with you from ECT mentors. It is a fitting way to end this book by hearing from people who are working most closely with ECTs. The range of advice and reflections will give you a lot to think about as you read the case studies.

In your own school, your ECT mentor and those working most closely with you will want to support you in any way they can and the hope is that this book will help you verbalise some of the ways that they can do this.

As the authors of this book, we want to recommend to you the supportive culture and fulfilling work in education. Both of us have enjoyed wonderful careers so far in primary teaching and in working with trainee teachers and ECTs. We wish you all the success you deserve and welcome you to the community of teaching.

Further reading

Suzanne Allies has a 'Supporting teacher well-being' website with lots of useful resources. Available at: www.supportingteacherwellbeing.wordpress.com (accessed 30 June 2022).

The Teacher Active website has put together some 'pro teaching tips'. Available at: https://blog.teacheractive.com/pro-teaching-tips-mistakes-ects-make-and-how-to-avoid-them (accessed 30 June 2022).

The Teachers' podcast interview with 'Mr T's NQTs' offers some reflections on engaging in the ECT framework and working with your ECT mentor. Available at: www.youtube.com/watch?v=WNv-Gh8FBiM (accessed 30 June 2022).

References

Adams, L (2021) Learning a New Skill Is Easier Said Than Done. [online] Available at: www.gordontraining.com/free-workplace-articles/learning-a-new-skill-is-easier-said-than-done/ (accessed 15 August 2022).

Allies, S (2021) *Supporting Teacher Well-being: A Practical Guide for Primary Teachers and School Leaders.* Abingdon: Routledge.

Covey, S (2004) *The 7 Habits of Highly Effective People.* New York: Free Press.

Day, C, Kington, A, Stobart, G and Sammons, P (2006) The Personal and Professional Selves of Teachers: Stable and Unstable Identities. *British Educational Research Journal*, 32(4): 601–16.

Deans for Impact (2022) *Practice with Purpose: The Emerging Science of Teacher Expertise.* [online] Available at: https://deansforimpact.org/resources/practice-with-purpose (accessed 2 July 2022).

Dweck, C (2017) *Mindset: Changing the Way You Think to Fulfil Your Potential.* London: Robinson.

Jacklin, A, Griffith, V and Robinson, C (2006) *Beginning Primary Teaching: Moving Beyond Surviving.* Maidenhead: Open University Press.

Lally, P, van Jaarsveld, C, Potts, H and Wardle, J (2010) How Are Habits Formed: Modelling Habit Formation in the Real World. *European Journal of Social Psychology*, 40(6): 998–1009.

Meijer, P, Korthagen, F and Vasalos, A (2009) Supporting Presence in Teacher Education: The Connection between the Personal and Professional Aspects of Teaching. *Teaching and Teacher Education*, 25(2): 297–308.

Paige, R, Geeson, R and Lambert, S (2020) *Building Skills for Effective Primary Teaching.* London: Learning Matters, Sage Publications.

Pierson, R (2013) *Every Child Needs a Champion.* [online] Available at: www.ted.com/talks/rita_pierson_every_kid_needs_a_champion?language=en (accessed 2 July 2022).

Price, S (2019) *Essential Guides for Early Career Teachers: Mental Well-being and Self-care.* St Albans: Critical Publishing.

Watts, E (ed) (1992) *Macbeth.* By Shakespeare, W. Ware: Wordsworth.

Acronym buster

Acronym	What does it stand for?	Notes/links
CPD	continuing professional development	
DfE	Department for Education	
DSL	designated safeguarding lead	
ECF	*Early Career Framework*	www.gov.uk/government/publications/early-career-framework
ECT	early career teacher	
EEF	Education Endowment Foundation	https://educationendowmentfoundation.org.uk
EHC	Education, health and care	
ESP	Education Support Partnership	www.educationsupport.org
ITT	Initial Teacher Training	
MAT	multi-academy trust	
NQT	newly qualified teacher	
PGCE	Post-Graduate Certificate of Education	
PPA	preparation, planning and assessment	
SATs	Standard Attainment Tests	Relating to the original name for these tests – now a colloquialism for these tests
SCITT	School Centred Initial Teacher Training	
SEN	Special Educational Needs	
SEND	Special Educational Needs and Disabilities	
SENDCo	Special Educational Needs and Disabilities Co-ordinator	
SLT	senior leadership team	
TA	teaching assistant	

Index

Note: Page numbers in **bold** and *italics* denote tables and figures, respectively